What People Are Saying About Justin Gary and *Think Like a Game Designer*

"*Think Like a Game Designer* should be on the shelf of anyone interested in game design, or even just in playing games. Plus, even people with no interest in games will learn valuable lessons about innovation, marketing, and how games motivate their players."

— **Ethan Mollick, Professor of Innovation and Entrepreneurship, Wharton School of Business**

"Justin has done a service to games by writing this book—even experienced designers will benefit from looking at design through his eyes."

— **Richard Garfield, Creator of *Magic: the Gathering*, *RoboRally*, and *King of Tokyo***

"Every journey starts with a single step, and if your desired journey is to become a game designer, I can think of no better first step than reading and doing the exercises in Justin's book. Justin has managed to capture and communicate the process for designing games starting from the blank sheet of paper all the way to thousands of fans playing your game."

— **Jordan Wiesman, Creator of *Shadowrun* and *BattleTech*, and Founder of WizKids game studio**

"Justin Gary went from world champion *Magic: The Gathering* pro-tour competitor to award-winning game designer and then to multi-million-dollar CEO. He has a lot to teach and you can find that wisdom clearly articulated in these pages."

— **Peter Adkinson, Founder of Wizards of the Coast and Owner of Gen Con, the largest tabletop gaming convention in North America**

"This book is not just for gamers. Anyone thinking about turning a skill or hobby into a successful career will benefit from Justin's experience and insight!"

— **Greg Goldstein, President and Publisher, IDW Publishing**

"Straightforward and relentlessly practical, this book efficiently guides you through the key steps involved in designing and publishing a game."

— **Raph Koster, Lead Designer of *Ultima Online* and Author of *A Theory of Fun for Game Design***

"Justin Gary has crafted a fun book that takes the essentials of game design and presents them in a light, personable format that anyone can understand. If you are new to game design, this is a great way to get started!"

— **Jesse Schell, CEO, Schell Games and Author of *The Art of Game Design***

"Justin Gary made one of my all-time favorite games. If you read his book, you might too."

— **Mike Selinker, CEO of LoneShark Games and creator of *Betrayal at House on the Hill***

"Anyone who wants to learn the ins and outs of game design will find no better source than this book by a true pro. Justin Gary takes you through everything from concept to final product, sharing examples from his own experiences. When you finish this book, you truly will think like a game designer."

— **Patrick Snow, Publishing Coach and International Best-Selling Author of *Creating Your Own Destiny* and *Boy Entrepreneur***

"Every page of *Think Like a Game Designer* is filled with truthful advice about the difficulties, joys, and most importantly, the processes of game design. Whether you want to design games, or you'd just like insight into how a creative mind works, you'll come away from this book seeing games in new ways."

— **Nicole Gabriel, Author of *Finding Your Inner Truth* and *Stepping Into Your Becoming***

"As an author, I thoroughly enjoyed learning how a game designer's mind works because I'm always open to new ways of being creative. This book is filled with useful nuggets of advice that are logical and applicable. If you want to take your love of games to the next level, there's no better place to start than here."

— **Tyler R. Tichelaar, PhD and Award-Winning Author of *Haunted Marquette* and *When Teddy Came to Town***

"Justin Gary seamlessly blends the art and science of game design into all of his work, and that's no different here. *Think Like a Game Designer* is an invaluable resource for game designers of all experience levels."

— **Patrick Sullivan, Senior Game Designer Dire Wolf Digital**

"Justin Gary has written a fantastic guide for aspiring game designers that not only walks them through the process of turning their idea into a finished game, but also teaches them how each step fits into the whole."

— **Paul Peterson, Senior Game Designer Plants vs. Zombies Heroes; Creator of** *Smash-Up Shufflebuilding Game*

"Justin Gary is a brilliant game designer and a great teacher. He has learned from experience and is awesome at breaking down the principles of design in ways that are easy to understand and act upon."

— **Rob Dougherty, Magic: the Gathering Hall of Fame; Founder and CEO White Wizard Games**

THINK LIKE A
GAME
DESIGNER

The Step-by-Step Guide to Unlocking Your Creative Potential

JUSTIN GARY

AVIVA
PUBLISHING

TO MY PARENTS

Mom, you are the best person I've ever met, and I was lucky enough to meet you on day one. You taught me love and compassion, and you inspired in me an insatiable curiosity and love of learning. You helped me believe in my ability to do anything, even when I couldn't do anything. I am living my dream life because of the lessons you instilled in me.

Dad, you are a force of nature. You taught me the value of following my passion and finding my own path. You showed me how to hustle and have an unparalleled zest for life. Our countless game nights inspired my love of play and are the reason I began the journey that led to this book.

CONTENTS

FOREWORD

I came *this* close to giving Justin his big break as a game designer. I first met Justin when he was a competitor in the *Magic: The Gathering* Junior Pro Tour. One of my many jobs back in the day was being liaison with the pro players, so I made sure to get to know everyone. Even as a teenager, Justin was one of the smartest players on the tour and he loved talking about games. It wasn't much later that, at age seventeen, he became the youngest player ever to become the *Magic: The Gathering* United States National Champion. Soon after, he and I became good friends.

Justin quickly advanced to the adult pro tour league, so I would see him about every other month always in a different city somewhere around the world. We would usually meet up for dinner after the pro tour and spend hours talking about various topics, usually games. I was impressed with his understanding of what made games tick and decided that as soon as he graduated from college, I was going to offer him a job at Wizards of the Coast (the company I work at that makes *Magic*).

Unfortunately, I wasn't alone. He got multiple offers, and much to my dismay, politely turned me down to go work at another game company. It was okay, though. I was a patient man, and I recognized the potential Justin had to offer. I could wait. Whenever I was in town, he and I would go out to dinner and Justin would show off his latest product that had been released. I was always impressed. My instincts hadn't been wrong. He was a great game designer.

Then one day, I learned that Justin was leaving the game company. I was finally going to have my chance to hire him. A day later, I learned he was starting his own company. Man, he wasn't making this easy. While I had great faith in Justin, the game industry is tough and starting a new company is quite the challenge. I wished him the best, but in the back of my head, I knew that, statistically speaking, I was probably going to have another chance to hire him. And then his company released its first game—*Ascension*. It went on to be a huge hit, and I finally realized that I'd missed my opportunity to hire Justin. He was going to be a giant success all on his own.

We still meet up for dinner when we're in the same city, and we still spend most of our time talking about games, but now I'm the one learning from him. This book is a chance for all of you to learn from him as well.

I've spent most of my adult life writing about game design, so I can spot when someone else shares the same skills. Justin not only understands how games tick, but he has the ability to communicate those ideas to everyone else. If you're interested in learning how to make games, or even if you already do and just want to do it better, this book's for you.

Let me end by congratulating Justin on his book. It's a wonderful accomplishment, one I'm happy you will get a chance to read (unless you're reading this in a bookstore, and if you are, come on—buy the damn thing!). I don't know if I could have predicted all those years ago that one day I'd be writing the foreword to his game design book, but really, if I thought about it, I should have.

But enough of me yapping, go read the book!

Sincerely,
Mark Rosewater

INTRODUCTION

"We know what we are, but know not what we may be."

— **William Shakespeare**

It was the biggest moment of my career, and I was ready to throw up.

Standing behind the stage at San Diego Comic Con, 2008, I peeked out behind the curtain to see 2,500 fans anxiously waiting for me to get on stage. The hum of the crowd permeated the room. I calmed my nerves before stepping out to announce my first major game design project: the *World of Warcraft Miniatures Game*.

This was the first time the public would see what I'd devoted more than three years of my life to creating. For me, this was the pinnacle of more than a decade I had spent in the gaming industry. Little did I know it was only the beginning....

If you are the kind of person who likes to play games, at some point you've probably thought, "Wouldn't it be sweet to make games for a living?" This book will show you how to do just that. It will also answer all of the common questions that come after: How do I get started? What if I get stuck? How do I get published? How do I make money? What if I'm not good enough?

I've been in the gaming industry for twenty years, and I've learned a lot along the way. I dropped out of law school with no idea how to make games, but I taught myself how to follow my passion.

In the process of writing this book, I've spoken with dozens of the world's best designers to learn more about the craft. I've found a remarkable consistency in how each person approaches design. Each designer brings his or her own style and methods to the process, but the underlying principles are universal. *There is a simple, learnable process for becoming a great game designer*, and I share that process in these pages.

Perhaps, like I did, you have apprehensions about being "creative." I first got my start in the game industry more than twenty years ago when I won the US National *Magic: The Gathering* Championships. For those who aren't familiar with it, *Magic: The Gathering* is a trading card game where players select from thousands of cards to build their own decks and compete against others. Think of it like a cross between chess and poker, where you get to select your own pieces at the start of the game. That championship launched a career that would take me around the world to tournaments in London, Sydney, Tokyo, and Rome. I made lifelong friendships and earned enough money to pay my way through college, while learning a ton about myself and the world around me. It was this tournament success that got me my first job as a developer for a Marvel vs. DC Comics trading card game.

I was hired because I was good at playing games, but I had no idea how to create them. In fact, I had never thought of myself as a "creative" guy. My approach was always analytical, breaking games down into their constituent parts so I could figure out how to win. It is this very process of breaking things down that led me to the principles I will share in this book and a profound insight: *There are no "creative people."* There are only people who follow this process in one form or another. The only prerequisite to being a game designer is a passion for making games and a willingness to do the work of iterative design. All the information you need to get started is available in this book.

Since beginning my career, I've started my own company, launched multi-million dollar games in both digital and tabletop form, and had the chance to work directly with some of the most brilliant minds in the industry. I've also made spectacular errors, faced near bankruptcy more than once, and am constantly learning from my mistakes. These pages contain lessons from both my successes and my failures so your learning process can be smoother than mine!

Teaching has always been a passion of mine. I firmly believe that the best way to master a subject is to teach it to others. I've lectured at schools and conventions. I've hired and trained designers using these methods. I've gotten everyone from grade-schoolers to senior citizens designing and creating their own games during a single two-hour class! After years of refinement, I've decided to codify these principles in writing so anyone can access them.

If you follow the step-by-step exercises in each chapter, you will be a game designer. Practicing and reviewing these principles with an open mind is all that stands between you and seeing your designs come to life. *These principles work.* And, as we'll see later in this book, they apply not just to making games, but to any creative endeavor. If you want to begin a career in game design, learn how to think like a game designer, or improve your thinking process for any creative challenge, this book has something for you.

In these pages, we will review everything from initial concept to final publication of a game in a way accessible to a novice, but with enough detail that even experienced designers will find value. I learned a lot in the process of writing this book, and it is my sincere hope that I will learn from all of you as you take these principles and expand on them in your own work. The community of game designers is a wonderful and inspiring one, and I am honored to welcome you to it. The process of learning a craft like game design is a lifelong one. I hope this book serves as a powerful touchstone on your journey.

PART I

Understanding Design

. . . .

CHAPTER 1

Learning Fundamentals

"Success is neither magical nor mysterious. Success is the natural consequence of consistently applying the basic fundamentals."

— **Jim Rohn**

WHAT IS A GAME DESIGNER?

Think back to a memorable game-playing experience from your past. Picture where you were and whom you were with. Take a moment and zoom in on what was going on in your experience that made it so memorable.

Were you able to snatch victory from the jaws of defeat (or vice-versa)?

Were you laughing and connecting with friends and loved ones?

Did you flip over the table in frustration?

Notice that whatever your particular story, the strong emotional reaction to the experience of play is what resonates with you today. That experience emerges from not just the game rules and components, but also from the environment, the people around you, and each player's background assumptions. A game designer's job is to craft that experience.

This job makes the broad definition of a game designer very simple: A game designer, like any other artist, aims to create an experience for the audience.

Games, however, have several unique features that separate them from other crafts. Those unique features are:

1. Games have players.
2. Games have rules.
3. Games are interactive.

These elements allow us to create a good starting point for a more precise definition of a game designer:

A game designer uses the interaction of players and rules to create an experience for the audience.

The audience is usually the players, but it can sometimes be viewers (e.g., at game shows, sports events, etc.). Many games are built with a viewing/streaming audience in mind, and e-sports are becoming a larger part of the gaming community each year. The same principles apply in either case, but in this book, we will assume your players are your audience.

WHAT MAKES A GREAT GAME DESIGNER?

To be a great game designer, you must be able to predict your players' emotional responses to the rules you design. Predictions require a degree of empathy and the ability to understand why people play games.

A great game designer must both predict the actions that players will take within a given game and understand how those actions will make players feel. To some of you, this definition may sound a bit wishy-washy.

"We have to talk about feelings?" Yup, there is no escaping it. *Our job as game designers can be described as working in a feeling factory.* Only by understanding our own feelings and emotional reactions to games can we empathize well enough with others to do our jobs well. Get ready to get uncomfortable!

HOW DO I BECOME A GREAT GAME DESIGNER?

Game designers become great through practice and attention. Three precursor habits need to be developed to become a great game designer:

1. Play lots of games.
2. Watch people play lots of games.
3. Bring awareness to the emotions that arise during play.

These habits will develop your intuition and improve your designs. Developing a habit of observing your players and taking in feedback (both explicit and implicit) will allow you to transform your initial concepts into great games.

WHERE DO I START?

No matter the type of game you eventually want to make, one of the best places to start learning the art of game design is through traditional board and card games.

The reason is those games have a very low iteration cost. You can try out an idea, test it, get feedback, and repeat the cycle with little overhead. This process allows you to learn what works and what doesn't, thus improving your design skills.

Playing games (even bad ones) is also valuable for learning more about game design. A great place to begin is with your favorite games. Figure out what about those games attracts you. *Pay attention to those moments when you notice yourself or other players having intense emotional responses (both good and bad).* Take note of what led to those emotions and think about how you could evoke them (or avoid them) in your own designs.

THE MOST IMPORTANT CONCEPT IN GAME DESIGN

The most important concept to understand as a game designer is what I call the core design loop. Every great designer uses this fundamental creative process in one form or another. Even if you think you are not creative, this process will get you creating in no time. The core design loop has six steps:

1. **Inspiring:** Decide what type of experience you will create.
2. **Framing:** Assess your parameters and deadlines.
3. **Brainstorming:** Get your ideas down on paper.
4. **Prototyping:** Bring your best ideas to life.
5. **Testing:** Learn what works and what doesn't.
6. **Iterating:** Use what you learned to improve the cycle.

As a general rule, the faster you can move through the above cycle (and the more iterations you get), the better your game will be. We will unpack all of those steps in detail in the upcoming chapters.

CHAPTER 2

Getting Started

"A journey of a thousand miles begins with one step."

— **Lao Tzu**

The goal of this book is to make you a *great* game designer. I've distilled here what I've learned from twenty years of experience along with takeaways from conversations with the best designers in the industry. We will get into the detailed tips and tricks of the trade, but first we have to get back to basics. This chapter is aimed at those who dream of designing games but haven't yet turned those dreams into reality. The most important step on this journey is the first one—getting started.

Why is it so hard to get started? Whether it's designing a game, starting a business, or any other creative endeavor, taking those first few steps always gets put off for "the right time" that never seems to come. No matter how many tips, tricks, or tactics you learn, something always gets in the way. Over time, you start to feel bad for not accomplishing your goals. The more your dreams get put off, the more shame and guilt you feel. The more shame you feel, the more you put off moving forward, in a terrible downward spiral.

Does this sound familiar? Why does this happen to us? The answer is *fear*.

Fear drives all of us. People often dismiss fear when there isn't immediate physical danger around, but that is a terrible mistake. Embarrassment and failure are far more common in our society than loss of life and limb, so they are rational fears. Don't be ashamed! You are not alone in facing fear; we all feel it! Even after years of success, accomplished designers still feel fear when starting something new and putting it out in front of others for the first time. The battle against fear is a lifelong one, and this chapter will give you the tools to wage that battle and win.

The first step to conquering fear is to name it. Fear is generated from the two building blocks of ego and uncertainty.

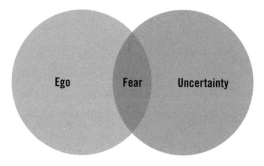

Let's take a look at each of these two challenges and how to overcome them.

EGO

How many times have you heard someone say, "I had that idea a while ago..." when you see some new game, invention, or company? How many times have you said that yourself?

Everyone has great ideas all the time. Everyone also has terrible ideas all the time. *When you expose your ideas to others, you risk finding out that your idea isn't really that good.* Try to think back on a time when you shared an idea or creative work and it got shot down. Do you remember how it felt? Did you shy back from sharing ideas like that in the future because of that feeling?

We wrap up our personal identity in our ideas. Most people think, *If my idea isn't good, neither am I.* Given that premise, it is no wonder most people protect their ideas from criticism! It is far easier to keep ideas locked up inside where they are safe than to expose them to testing and see what really works and what doesn't. *By never trying, you never risk anything.*

HOW TO OVERCOME EGO

The key to battling your ego is to disentangle the value of your ideas from your own self-worth. Let go of the attachment to any idea as "yours." Imagine instead that your ideas have been proposed by a stranger. If you think the idea is a good one, then it is your job to try it out and see how it might be improved even further, but it isn't a judgment on you if the idea is bad. When I look to hire a game designer, I am far happier to hire someone who puts out twenty bad ideas and two good ones than someone who doesn't come up with any. In fact, it is most often the bad ideas that become the seeds for future good ideas!

The best designers take ideas from all around them and are constantly trying things that don't work. In fact, as we will discuss later, the only way to be a designer is to spend a lot of time trying things that don't work! *Stop identifying with your ideas and start identifying with this process.* Then you will be on your way to thinking like a designer.

EXERCISE

Write down a list of ten new game ideas. Don't spend too much time thinking about each one or worrying about whether the ideas are "good." Just generate ideas and write them down. Go ahead; I'll wait. This exercise shouldn't take more than ten minutes, and it will help you get past the fear of writing bad ideas. The very act of writing down bad ideas will help you create good ones in the future and get you used to the idea of being creative.

_____

_____

_____

_____

_____

_____

_____

_____

_____

_____

Bonus: Repeat this exercise every day for the next week. Keep your lists because they will come in handy later.

UNCERTAINTY

Humans are lazy by nature. The brain uses over 20 percent of the body's energy, so conserving mental resources makes sense. This conservation served us well during our evolution as a species. Why waste precious energy on tasks when we don't need to? In particular, why spend time on an uncertain task when we could instead choose something more predictable? Stick with what you know and you can reliably get through the day—or so we think.

Sticking to routine can be a great thing if you already have the life you want, but if you want to achieve great things (like designing awesome games for a living), you are going to have to leave your comfort zone and start facing uncertainty head on.

Creativity is by definition uncertain. *The act of being creative is essentially nothing more than combining things that haven't been combined before.* Doing things that haven't been done before is scary! Looking at an end goal (e.g., a published game) that seems so far away and nebulous creates a sickening feeling in the stomach, so the instinct is to turn quickly to something less scary like watching cat videos on YouTube. Even if you can figure out how to get it done, it is uncertain whether the end product will be anything like what you envision. Many questions and fears are likely to pop up as you contemplate a new design:

- Where do I even start?

- Will anyone want to buy this?

- What if it doesn't work?

- How will I get this made?

- Can I do this?

These are fine questions to have, but you can't expect to answer them all before you even get started. You need to be comfortable with some uncertainty, even as you take small steps to move forward to bring your vision to life.

HOW TO OVERCOME UNCERTAINTY: START SMALL

"You don't have to see the whole staircase to take the first step."

— **Martin Luther King, Jr.**

The first step to overcoming uncertainty is to start small. One of the best approaches is simply to ask yourself, "What is the next action I can take to move forward?" A big amorphous project like building a new game is intimidating, but one next step isn't. Don't believe me? Try this exercise: Pick any project you want to do but have been putting off. It doesn't need to be a giant, life-changing thing, but it can be if you want. Maybe it's cleaning out the garage, planning a trip, or learning the guitar. Notice what emotions come up when you think of it.

Now, think of the very next physical activity you need to do to move that project forward. Maybe it's looking up a tutor online, calling a friend to ask about available dates, or picking up cleaning supplies from the store. Commit to doing just that one small next step within the next forty-eight hours. Notice what emotions come up now. As you complete the exercise, if you like, think about the next small thing you would need to do and commit to that. As you build momentum, even giant-seeming tasks can be chipped away.

The instructions in this book are designed to provide small, actionable tasks that will move you forward in the process of creating your first game. Commit to doing these exercises, and just take them one at a time, without worrying too much about the end goal. If you take this step-by-step approach, you will be designing games in no time.

ACCEPT IMPERFECTION

"If you look for perfection, you'll never be content."

— Leo Tolstoy

I'm sorry to be the bearer of bad news, but your first game is going to suck. Please understand I'm not saying this to disparage you. I'm just sharing a basic fact that is as true for you as it is for me and every great designer I know. *Only the people who make games that suck then move on to create something awesome.*

Nobody starts out as an expert. It is the very process of trying, failing, learning, and then trying again that is the heart of good design. We will go through the core design loop in detail later in the book so you have a step-by-step guide for how to do it.

In order to go through this loop, however, you have to be willing to fail. This isn't just a concern for beginners. I can look back at any period of my design history and find elements I'm not proud of. This has been true for every designer I've spoken with, and I'm confident it will remain true for me for the totality of my career.

Embracing imperfection will remove the fear of not doing it "right." Strive to do your best with every project, but let go of the need to be perfect. *Done is better than perfect.*

THE ONE MAGICAL SOLUTION TO FEAR: SET DEADLINES

"The ultimate inspiration is the deadline."

— Nolan Bushnell

If there is one trick that has had an enormous impact on my game design career, it is this: Set deadlines.

When I first started designing games, I was working for someone else, building games for major properties like Marvel Comics and World of Warcraft. I was given deadlines to complete my designs, and I got them done. Keep in mind that I had no experience designing games and no idea what I was doing! But knowing that I had a deadline, and that I would not keep my job if I missed those deadlines, forced me to focus on doing the work.

Deadlines are magical. *Deadlines force you to focus on the essential and commit to getting things done.* Think about how efficiently you work when you are about to leave for vacation. Your productivity skyrockets because you know you have to get things done and are excited about the end result. It is easy to let a "side project" like designing a game or writing a book constantly slip in favor of more pressing demands. Set a reasonable but aggressive deadline and stick to it.

It can be very helpful to tell other people about your deadline to increase the pressure (e.g., set up a game night in two weeks with some friends to test your first prototype, or commit to posting a chapter a week of your book online).

I won't lie to you. Even with the above tips, getting started is still going to be difficult. In fact, it is this very challenge that makes the project worth doing! Completing a creative project brings with it its own rewards even if it isn't "The Next Big Thing." *You learn from everything you do*, and you get to express yourself (flaws and all) with each project you complete.

Be bold, take risks, and have fun! Succeed or fail, you will be in good company.

EXERCISE

"Eighty percent of success is showing up."

— Woody Allen

So that is it. I want you to commit—*right now*—to the first steps of becoming a game designer. Write down below what you intend with a deadline attached. The steps can be finishing this book and its exercises, landing a job as a game designer, completing your first game, or publishing your twentieth game. It's up to you! Pick realistic but exciting goals that you can complete within the next year.

1. _____

Deadline: _____

2. _____

Deadline: _____

3. _____

Deadline: _____

4. _____

Deadline: _____

5. _____

Deadline: _____

For extra power, post the above commitment in a public forum. You can even let me know what you are up to on Twitter @Justin_Gary. Making a commitment public makes it more real and adds some healthy social pressure to get it done. If you are anything like me, you love reading books about how to get things done, but you often find yourself finishing them without taking action. This exercise will break you of that habit. Before turning to the next page, take five minutes to solidify your intention and tell it to the world. Step 1 in getting started is: *Take action now!*

CHAPTER 3

Overcoming Obstacles

"Everyone has a plan until they get punched in the face."

— Mike Tyson

We have one more piece of psychological housekeeping to do before we get into the nuts and bolts of design. If you followed the steps in the last section, then you are already on your way to designing games. Congratulations! If you haven't started yet, that's okay, but take a second to think about why and perhaps schedule a time soon to get started on doing and not just reading.

Once you've gotten started, you will inevitably hit barriers and obstacles along the way. Life has a funny way of not turning out as we planned. During the hustle of your everyday life, it is easy to let your goals fall by the wayside. How can we overcome these daily obstacles and be ready for when life punches us in the face?

KNOW YOUR WHY

"Obstacles are those frightful things you see when you take your eyes off your goal."

— Henry Ford

When working on a game, things get frustrating. It can often feel like you are taking two steps backward for each step forward. As you work, other priorities will get in the way. Taking care of chores, working your day job, and surfing the internet will all vie for your attention. *How do you stay motivated? The answer is to find your why.*

Knowing your why and keeping it visible is a powerful tool for staying on track. You need a visible, visceral reminder of why something is important to you to give you enough motivation to push through setbacks along the way. We all have different whys, and you should be honest with yourself about what yours is. When you are designing a game, are you making it so you can express yourself? Do you want to quit your job and do something you are passionate about? Do you want to show off how clever you are?

Whatever your reasons, it is important to make those reasons visceral and keep them in mind so you don't lose your way.

KEEP YOUR GOALS VISIBLE

Setting concrete goals and keeping them in front of you will remind you what you are working toward. I keep a Post-it note on my computer with my immediate goals and keep a digital list of long-term goals that I review regularly. Each of my short-term goals has a deadline attached to it. Think about where you can keep your goals written down so you will see them regularly. If you are anything like me, most of your life is lived on screens, be they phone, computer, or tablet. Even though digital lists are valuable (and I use them regularly), I recommend trying a non-digital goal list. Digital lists can often get eclipsed by the many distractions created by phones and the internet. A physical list in a visible place can be a powerful reminder of what you are working toward.

ASK "WHAT'S NEXT?"

If you find yourself getting stuck on a goal, try breaking it down into smaller chunks until you find something you can start making progress on. "Design and publish a miniatures game" may be an intimidating goal, but "Brainstorm combat mechanics for twenty minutes" is far more manageable. In the section on how to get started, we talked about the value of "starting small," and this is an extension on that advice. Once you get moving, momentum can help you get past additional obstacles.

ASK FOR HELP

> "If you cannot see where you are going, ask someone who has been there before."
>
> **— J. Loren Norris**

Successful people are not afraid to ask for help when they need it. Most people in the gaming industry are friendly and happy to help someone who asks good questions. Great resource sites exist on the web where you can ask questions about almost anything. If that doesn't work, reaching out to friends or potential mentors in the industry is a great approach.

When approaching a potential mentor, make it clear that you've done your homework. Don't ask a question that a quick Google search could solve. Be specific with your questions and respectful of people's time.

Online communities like Quora and Reddit are invaluable for sustaining your momentum and finding support. Keep making progress every day and you'll be amazed by what you can accomplish.

EXERCISE

Think about your end goal. Why do you want to design games? What is the end goal you are trying to achieve? Take a moment to visualize what it will be like to complete your goal. Try to imagine the details of what it will feel like, look like, and even smell like to have a completed game you are proud of. Make each experience as real and visceral as possible. Now write down a brief description of your end goal. If needed, break down that goal by writing down the next small action to take to reach it.

My Why:

_____

_____

_____

_____

_____

_____

PART II

Learning the Core Design Loop

. . . .

CHAPTER 4

The Steps of the Core Design Loop

Now that we've gotten personal psychology out of the way, it's time to unpack the most important concept in game design. Let's dig into the "core design loop." Following are the six steps for successfully designing a game.

Step 1: Inspiring
Step 2: Framing
Step 3: Brainstorming
Step 4: Prototyping
Step 5: Testing
Step 6: Iterating

The skill of game design is to go through the core design loop as quickly and efficiently as possible until you reach a finished product. This section will go into detail about each phase and includes exercises to get you moving through your first design loop.

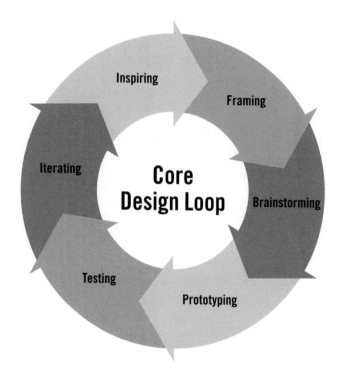

"Learn the rules like a pro, so you can break them like an artist."

— **Pablo Picasso**

When you first start this process, I recommend taking the time to go through each step completely so you can get familiar with it. After you gain experience going through the loop a few times, you'll be able to use shortcuts and modifications that suit your particular working style.

CHAPTER 5

Inspiring

"The best way to have a good idea is to have lots of ideas."

— Linus Pauling

Everything starts with an idea. To create a game, you need at least a vague concept of what you want to bring into the world. You may already have dozens of ideas you want to bring to life, but you aren't sure how. Or you may find even the thought of "being creative" and coming up with a game idea is intimidating. Maybe for you, inspiration sounds like something that happens when you forget to put on deodorant.

This chapter will bring inspiration down to earth. *Everyone can be inspired and everyone can be creative.* Despite all the hype to the contrary, inspiration is both the easiest *and* least important part of the design process.

Here are three fundamental truths that level the playing field:

1. Everyone Has Great Ideas

Everybody has great ideas all the time. Most people simply don't take the time to write down those ideas or develop them into something amazing. Being creative is about learning to trust yourself enough to put work into testing and refining your ideas until they become real. Following the steps below will help you capture and develop your hidden inspiration.

2. Ideas Are 10 Percent. Execution Is 90 Percent.

A mediocre idea for a game executed well can be a big success. A brilliant idea executed poorly rarely is. Don't feel like your idea needs to be "the next big thing" before you can start working on it. *Great ideas are force multipliers for your work.* It is worth spending time trying to find and cultivate them. But don't let the fetishization of ideas block you from moving forward on bringing your own ideas to life.

A good idea is a critical foundation upon which to build a game (or a company, or anything else), but *the heart of creative work is execution.* There are two ways to think about this. On the one hand, it's a bummer that you can't just think of a good idea and make a million dollars. That would be a lot easier than the hard work of bringing an idea to life!

On the other hand, this realization is empowering. *There is no magic or genius "out there" that you don't have.* You can make a great game, found a great company, or create a great product. All it takes is the willingness to do the work of execution. There are always roadblocks to overcome. The path to bringing ideas to life will often cause them to change far beyond what you initially conceive. *Get in the habit of capturing and testing your ideas.* Avoid the habit of cherishing them so much that they cannot be scrutinized or changed. That is how brilliant ideas turn into brilliant realities.

3. Every Great Idea Is a Rip Off of Another Great Idea

"Creativity is knowing how to hide your sources."

— C. E. M. Joad (regularly credited to Albert Einstein)

All creation is theft. Creativity is taking concepts you have encountered before and combining them in new and innovative ways. *Nothing is completely original.* The most successful games in the world are a product of this process. *Magic: The Gathering* combined the customized role selection of *Cosmic Encounters* with a *Dungeons and Dragons* theme and cards. *League of Legends* combined *Warcraft 3* with fan mods focusing on heroes instead of troops. Each of these games grosses hundreds of millions of dollars a year!

Don't be afraid to borrow liberally from other creative works you admire. The key to creative design is to unite two concepts and present them in a way that creates a new experience. If you let your creative interests guide your decisions, your authentic voice cannot help but speak through the designs you create.

GENERATING IDEAS: ABE (ALWAYS BE EXPLORING)

So now that we've taken some of the mystery out of ideas, let's look at a step-by-step process for generating ideas of your own.

The key to finding good inspiration is to *have a lot of raw material* to draw from. The more games you play, the more grist for the mill of creativity you will have. *To create things that are interesting, be interested.*

Pay attention and follow your curiosity.

Try and figure out how things tick.

Seek a deep understanding of the world.

Play lots of games. Even games you don't like!

Inspiration can come from anywhere—not just games. Explore your passions in unrelated industries. Do you love sewing? How could the mechanics of sewing be turned into a game? Perhaps an exotic destination you travel to can provide the setting for your next game. Even experiences you hate can provide inspiration. Next time you are stuck in traffic, think about making a "racing" game where you race to work at rush hour. Is there a rage meter you have to manage to survive the trip?

Inspiration is all around us, and as a designer, you need to train your eye to pull out the little elements that make games (and other aspects of life) tick.

DON'T FORGET THE HUNAN BEEF

One of the most powerful habits to develop as a designer is to keep a journal. As you go about your day, jot down things that interest you and write down problems you want to solve. Take down notes whenever you think of them and review them regularly.

Most good ideas are lost because people don't write them down. Trust me, you don't want to be in this position. To illustrate, I will share a story from when my team and I were developing the digital card game *SolForge*. We were brainstorming designs for our second set of cards, and we were on a roll. Ideas were flowing, and by the time we finished the multi-hour meeting, we all felt like we had a great direction for the project. These team brainstorms can be mentally draining, and a few hours in, we were all getting pretty hungry. I noticed one member of our team writing things down, and eventually, we took a break, ordered some food, and moved on to other projects.

A few days later, we were trying to remember the specific mechanics we had come up with and had forgotten quite a bit. I recalled that one team member had written things down (my team is well trained), so I looked for the notepad he had been working on and began to read aloud to the team:

Hunan Beef

Kung Pao Chicken

Fried Rice....

I realized with horror that this list was clearly not notes from our brainstorm. Instead, the paper contained a combination of doodles and fantasizing about the upcoming Chinese food lunch order. We had to start from scratch on our *SolForge* designs. Around the office, we now have a shorthand for when someone needs to start taking notes during a brainstorm: Hunan Beef.

DON'T BE AFRAID TO SHARE YOUR IDEAS

Ideas are important, but not as important as everyone thinks. Think of your game idea as the foundation for a house. If it isn't solid, the house is in trouble. On the other hand, without all the planning, labor, and resources required to build an actual house, all you have is an empty lot. Sharing your idea early helps you make sure you have a good foundation before investing in building your house.

I've encountered multiple designers who were terrified that someone would steal their brilliant game concept. So terrified, in fact, that they never showed it to anyone. Those game ideas may have been brilliant, but no one will ever know because they never saw the light of day. The iterative design process requires constant testing and feedback. This is true even before you build your first prototype. If you don't show your ideas to others and get input, you are unlikely to make it far. Adopt an abundance mentality when it comes to ideas. You will always have more, so don't be afraid to share them liberally.

THEME VS. MECHANICS

A common divide in the game design community is between designers who get their inspiration primarily from the game's theme (the story) or the game's mechanics (the rules). There is no right and wrong in how you answer this question. Inspiration can come from anywhere, so you should not feel the need to follow one path or another.

While I am generally a "mechanics first" designer, I find it helpful to think about themes ahead of time, and I almost always have one in mind when I start a project. It is very likely that both your theme and your mechanics will shift as you go through the design loop, so just pick whatever gets you excited the most and start down that path. I will talk about theme development more in Chapter 16: Polish.

EXERCISE

This exercise is broken down into six twenty-minute chunks. Each should be done in order, but they don't need to be done all at once.

1. Review the Games You Love

Hopefully, if you are interested in designing games, you've played a lot of them. Find what got you passionate about gaming in the first place and bring it to your first creations. Use the space below or take a piece of paper and create as long a list as possible of your favorite games and gaming genres. Spend at least twenty minutes on this, and try to make your list as complete as possible. Include games you played as a child and categories of play you wouldn't generally think of (video games, board games, role-playing games, drinking games, etc.).

_____

_____

_____

_____

_____

_____

2. Review the Games You Hate

Any game that has some popularity has something to teach you and some core elements that may be valuable in design. Think about popular games you've played or games your friends play that haven't hit the mark for you. Take a few minutes and add this list below:

_____

_____

_____

_____

_____

_____

3. Find the Gems

Spend time thinking more granularly than a player does. What features of your favorite games really bring them to life for you? What mechanics, components, themes, and external factors lead to the experiences and feelings you most enjoyed?

Can you find any great features even in the games you hate? Create a new list of as many of these elements as possible, and highlight the ones that most intrigue you. Pay close attention to your intense feelings during play—try to identify what about the game triggered those emotions.

_____

_____

_____

_____

_____

_____

4. Find the Crud

Now think about the elements you don't like. Don't look just at games you don't like overall, but look for ways that the games you love fail. Think about ways that those games could be better. New designers have a tendency to want to add components to their favorite games, but think also about what could be subtracted. The best designers are focused not on adding new things, but on removing what gets in the way of the core design. Add this list of crud below.

_____

_____

_____

_____

_____

_____

5. Look for Patterns

If you've followed the above steps, you should have a long list of games you love and games you don't love as much. You also have a list of specific mechanics that you love or don't

love. Glance over these lists to see what jumps out at you. Is
there anything you can combine that hasn't been combined
before? Is there anything you can remove to make a game
more successful? Spend twenty minutes jotting down game
concept ideas that are one or two sentences long. Don't censor
yourself; just keep writing during this period so you can get
as many ideas on paper as possible. If you stop moving your
pen for more than thirty seconds, you are doing it wrong.

_____

_____

_____

_____

_____

_____

6. Pick Your Favorite Concept and Start Working on It

The next steps of the core design loop concern beginning to refine your concept and bring it to life. Choose one
of the ideas above and use it to take you through the next
steps of the design loop. *Get yourself into a state where you can
prototype and test as quickly as possible so you can start learning
and improving.*

CHAPTER 6

Framing

"Cinema is a matter of what's in the frame and what's out."

— **Martin Scorsese**

Framing is the process of defining the space within which you will work. One of the biggest challenges of designing a game can be how open-ended the process feels. Limitless possibility is intimidating! It may seem counter-intuitive, but the best way to be creative is to give yourself restrictions.

CREATE MORE BY CHANGING LESS

Game systems are delicate creatures. Changing one part can have ripple effects on the whole design. Deciding to hold some things constant at each step of the process allows you to be more effective with the changes you do make. Staring at a blank page with no limitations can be very daunting, but knowing you want to make a $14.99 retail price card game for 8-12 year olds or a first-person shooter video game using only stick figure characters can immediately start you down a path. *Limitations breed creativity.*

BE YOUR OWN BOSS

One of the benefits of being hired to design games is that framing is often done for you. You are told who your game is for, what the theme will be, and when the game needs to be complete. These frames do a wonderful job of focusing your attention on what really matters. When you are designing games on your own, you need to be your own boss and define these parameters for yourself.

While framing, you need to ask three fundamental questions. Hold on to the answers to these questions through your first design cycle. You can change them later if need be, but *there is value in wrestling with limitations before you relax them.*

FRAMING QUESTION 1: WHO IS YOUR TARGET AUDIENCE?

While we all would love to design games enjoyed by everyone, you need to pick a smaller target to aim at during design. *If you are trying to design something for everyone, you are really not designing for anyone.* What key attributes define members of your ideal player group? Try to think about their ages, hobbies, and interests. Create a mental picture in your mind of someone in this group. Use questions to clarify that picture.

- What activities does he or she engage in?

- What motivates him or her?

- What types of things does he or she buy?

- What kinds of games does he or she play now?

- Why does he or she play those games?

Answering these questions and keeping a mental picture of your target audience in your head will help guide your design process. Don't try to make your audience too broad, especially at first. Keep your focus small. Envision one member of your target audience and design a game for him or her specifically. The easiest target audience to design for is yourself. Creating games that you yourself love to play has the wonderful advantage of being obvious when you succeed or fail.

Even if you are targeting yourself, make sure you find others who also fall within your target audience to playtest your game and provide feedback. We are often blind to our own shortcomings, so only the harsh reality of playtesters outside of your design team can give you the feedback you need.

FRAMING QUESTION 2: WHAT IS YOUR HOOK?

"If you can't explain it simply,
you don't understand it well enough."

— Albert Einstein

Every great game has a hook. Each year, hundreds of games are released and available online and on store shelves. What makes yours stand out? There are lots of possible answers to this question, and hopefully, you have developed yours during the inspiration step, but it's worth thinking about the question and writing down explicit answers.

The business concept of the "elevator pitch" is useful here. Imagine that you just so happen to be in an elevator with a wealthy investor. You only have a minute to convince this person that you are worth his time after the doors open.

How would you do this? There are many approaches, but the easiest is to *connect two exciting things in a unique way* (e.g., *Angry Birds* with *Star Wars* characters, a digital trading card game plus a tactical RPG (role-playing game), a deckbuilding game using dice instead of cards, etc.).

The same principle will apply with your customer as he browses past your game in a store or ad. *How would you describe your game in one or two sentences?* What differentiates it from other games? I don't mean that the entire game needs to be described in two sentences—just the unique hook that gets someone interested. If answering this question takes more than two sentences, you need to refine further.

FRAMING QUESTION 3: WHAT ARE YOUR EXTERNAL RESTRICTIONS?

"I don't need time. What I need is a deadline."

— Duke Ellington

Every design process has restrictions—some more severe than others. Think about what you must work around and what will constrain your design. Do you have a deadline? Do you have a brand or intellectual property you have to design for? Do you have cost limitations? Do you have a programming language or platform you must use?

As counter-intuitive as it is, even if you are designing for yourself and have no immediate restrictions of time and cost, it is helpful to create artificial restrictions. Remember, limitations breed creativity. *Placing deadlines on yourself forces you to focus on what matters.* This focus helps you to move a game forward rapidly, rather than endlessly refining, tweaking, and procrastinating. Write down your restrictions and use them as guidance for the next phase.

Parameters you create are not set in stone, but they are going to help you through the rest of your first design cycle. Holding some variables constant will drive your creativity and move you quickly into the prototype phase.

EXERCISE

Using your design inspiration in Part I, answer the three questions above and set a deadline for completing a playable prototype!

Who is my target audience?

_____

What is my hook?

_____

_____

What are my external restrictions?

_____

_____

_____

What deadline will I commit to for my first prototype?

_____

CHAPTER 7

Brainstorming

"Creativity is allowing yourself to make mistakes.
Art is knowing which ones to keep."

— Scott Adams

Brainstorming is my favorite part of the game design process. If you've followed the exercises up to this point, you have a core inspiration and a set of initial parameters for your game. If so, congratulations! You are now ready to brainstorm.

If you haven't followed any exercises, take a second to ask yourself, "Why?" What feelings are you experiencing and what is driving your behavior? For some people, reading through the book first is a better way to learn. This is especially true if you are an experienced designer and already have some form of this process in place. But for most people, putting off doing the exercises is just another way to procrastinate rather than do the work and take risks. Be honest with yourself before moving forward. At the very least, the exercise of analyzing your feelings and motivations is great practice for the core skill of being a game designer!

In this chapter, we are going to use your inspiration and frame to generate a staggering number of ideas in a very short period of time. The brainstorming process is broken down into three phases:

1. **Creation:** Generate as many ideas as possible.
2. **Organization:** Organize those ideas and look for patterns.
3. **Elimination:** Pick one core idea to prototype.

Each phase requires a very different mode of thinking, so it's important to do each one in order. Most people are more inclined toward one type of thinking or another, so as you go through the below steps, keep an eye on where your mind wanders (e.g., analytical folk like myself always look for what's wrong and often go to the elimination stage too early). As you notice these tendencies, try to resist the urge to jump to your preferred mode of thinking. After you've got some experience doing brainstorming on your own, it can help to find other people to collaborate with who have different inclinations. Your respective strengths will complement each other. I'll talk more about group brainstorming below.

PHASE 1: CREATION

"Create something today even if it sucks."

— Unknown

During the first phase of brainstorming, *the goal is to get as many ideas down on paper as possible.* During this phase, my motto is: "There are no bad ideas." Everything is fair game.

Use your initial inspiration and frame as a jumping-off point, but let your mind go wild from there. Each idea you write down will spawn other ideas that will, in turn, spawn even more. Continue to write things down for the entirety of your allotted time.

Even if one of your ideas is totally impractical (e.g., This game requires zero gravity to play), it may help lead you to an innovative solution you hadn't thought of (e.g., I could use magnets as game pieces that repel each other). Even if you have one idea for how a specific part of your game will work, keep writing until you come up with three or four more—you want to get past the obvious solution and dig for hidden treasures in your psyche.

If you stop writing for more than twenty seconds, you are being too critical with your ideas. If you hear that voice in your head saying, "That will never work!" or "That's stupid!" just tell the voice to be quiet and stand in the corner. You'll have plenty of chance to let your inner critic loose later. Don't let your judgmental mind restrict your creative mind during this phase.

It may help you to think of this as play. Nobody but you will see these ideas, and it's okay to be as ridiculous as you want. Have fun with it!

EXERCISE

Brainstorm around your game inspiration. Take twenty minutes and begin your brainstorm process. Use the below lines, but take an extra sheet of paper if needed! Remember not to restrict yourself when coming up with ideas. The more ideas you generate at this phase, the better the rest of the process will be. Allow yourself to be wrong and ridiculous! When you finish this phase, you should have a massive list of ideas in a random jumble on your page—ready to be organized into something useful.

_____

_____

_____

_____

_____

_____

PHASE 2: ORGANIZATION

After finishing phase one, you should have a giant list of ideas on paper in front of you. Now, step back and look at the whole image. Let your mind find patterns between the different ideas and start to group them together into like categories.

Mind mapping tools are incredibly helpful here. Mind mapping is just a fancy phrase for writing out your ideas in a way that highlights their connections. To create a mind map, simply identify a few primary "idea bubbles" and draw a circle around them. Then, start drawing in lines to new ideas that connect to your original bubbles. There are no hard and fast rules, but in the end, your mind map should look something like this:

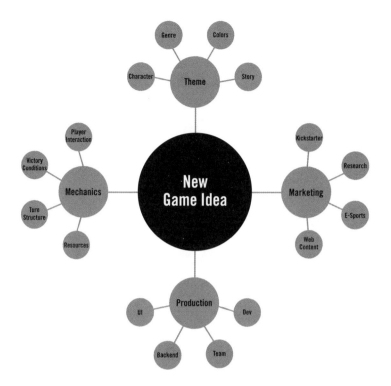

You can find many free digital tools to help you mind map (I use FreeMind and WorkFlowy), but classic pen and paper work just fine. A whiteboard is also great for this. If using pen and paper, I recommend using a big sheet (or maybe two sheets) to ensure you have enough room for all your ideas. As silly as it seems, when a paper starts getting cramped and filled up with writing, it sends a subtle cue to your brain to stop generating new ideas. Big white space encourages big ideas.

There are many ways to group ideas in a mind map, but here are a few that work well for games:

- Core Mechanics
- Setup
- Theme

- Resources

- Components

- Turn Structure

- Victory Conditions

- Level Concepts

- Story Ideas

You may also have crazier categories for ideas like: Requires Nuclear Fission, Solid Gold Psychic Aliens, Edible Game Pieces, etc. Again, there are no wrong answers here.

As you organize, other ideas will come to you to fill in the gaps in the categories you are building. Go ahead and add those in as well. Look for ways to connect where you are now to some of the ideas you've written down. Some great questions to ask include:

- How would you get from here to there?

- What other components would need to exist?

- How would a player experience this idea?

EXERCISE

Take your creation list from the above exercise and create a mind map of your ideas.

Just like with the first exercise, spend at least twenty minutes on this phase. Use that time to scan over the map and find ideas you may not have thought of originally. When you finish this phase, you should have a relatively organized set of concepts. Some of these ideas will be great, some crazy, some unfinished, and some will be close to executable. You are now ready for the final phase of brainstorming.

PHASE 3: ELIMINATION

Here is where your inner critic returns. Start filtering through the ideas and find the core elements that can be prototyped. *While your goal in phase one was to generate as many ideas as possible, your goal in phase three is to prototype as few things as possible.* Ask yourself what the best part of your design is and figure out the cheapest, fastest way to test it.

We will talk more about prototyping in the next chapter, but its key principle is to try to test your assumptions in the form of real gameplay as quickly and efficiently as you can. Don't worry at this point about leaving great ideas on the table. You can always come back to them in the next cycle. You are trying to find the gem that will form the heart of your design and the minimum number of additional items required to test and iterate on that gem.

EXERCISE

Pick a single focus to prototype.

Take a look at your mind map and find the single core idea that excites you the most. Think through the minimum number of components you need to test that idea and jot down that idea and those components below. Write out everything you need to test out the core idea. If the list doesn't fit below, you probably need to refine it further. You will use this idea to begin prototyping in the next chapter.

_____

_____

_____

_____

_____

Note: I recommended setting aside twenty minutes for each of the above exercises. If you feel like you are on a roll and want to run over, that is okay! But don't spend less than twenty minutes on each phase. This time is critical because each phase uses a very different part of your brain, and it takes time to ramp up to maximum efficiency. One of the main advantages of brainstorming is finding the ideas hiding in your psyche, so take the time to do it, even if you think you already have "the answer."

RULES FOR GROUP BRAINSTORMING

Group brainstorming can be a great way to get more ideas than you would ever come up with on your own. However, several risks are associated with a group brainstorm. *Finding the right people and enforcing the right kind of discipline are key components of making the most out of a group brainstorm.* I recommend you go through the brainstorming process individually before bringing in a group so you have a sense of what to expect.

1. Start with a Few Minutes of Individual Brainstorming.

Before beginning a group brainstorm, give everyone individual time to think of ideas. It's easy to become enrolled in someone else's idea before you have a chance to generate your own. Even a few minutes of personal brainstorming at the start of a session can yield valuable concepts that would have been drowned out in a group.

2. Make Sure Everyone Understands the "No Bad Ideas" Rule for the Creation Phase.

If the group members support each other in creating more and more ideas, then a group brainstorm session can be a huge asset. If, however, people are afraid to say ideas for fear of looking stupid or being embarrassed, they will self-edit, and then you can miss a lot of great ideas. The best designers are those who will shout out ten bad ideas to find one good one. Don't crush that instinct by making fun of the bad ideas before the good one can show up. Create a culture of inclusion and make the process fun!

3. Make Ideas Visible

As ideas are shouted out, write them on a white board or some other large, visible medium. Seeing the brainstorm in front of you helps you stay focused, and written down ideas are more likely to spawn new ideas.

One great tactic for incorporating all of the above is to give your team members sticky notes and have them write down their ideas individually for ten minutes, only then adding the ideas to the wall and using them to spawn more group ideas. Keep group brainstorms small (2-6 people) to encourage participation and prevent people from "hiding" in a larger group.

To learn how to apply these principles to group brainstorming in a fun and effective way, check out *The Breakthrough Game*, which I co-created in partnership with the Wharton School of Business. You can find it at www.TheBreakthroughGame.com.

EXERCISE

Get together with a group of like-minded designers or game enthusiasts (no more than six total) and practice the above steps in a group brainstorm or Breakthrough Game session. Write down your top takeaways from the group brainstorm on the lines below. Pay attention to what worked and what didn't in your group brainstorm session and make notes for how to improve in the future.

_____

_____

_____

_____

_____

CHAPTER 8

Prototyping

"It doesn't matter how beautiful your theory is, it doesn't matter how smart you are. If it doesn't agree with experiment, it's wrong."

— **Richard Feynman**

No matter how great a designer you are, you will never know whether your game is good until you prototype and test it. *The goal of prototyping is to test out a core game concept as quickly and cheaply as possible.* You should have your core concept from your brainstorm session before beginning to prototype.

THE BASICS

So what is a prototype? *A prototype is a simplified version of your game, intended to test a core mechanic or feature.* As you test different ideas, your prototype will get more and more refined until eventually you feel comfortable creating the game's final version.

A prototype is composed of three elements:

1. Rules
2. Components

3. Questions

Let's review each of these elements briefly.

RULES

You should have a written set of rules for your game. In early iterations, these rules can be in shorthand and verbally told to players. Even in the earliest stages, however, write down your rules! Being able to refer back to older rules as you test and iterate is invaluable. You will be shocked by what you forget if you don't write things down.

I'm serious—write down your rules! I've made the Hunan Beef mistake too many times.

COMPONENTS

Components are the items needed for physically playing the game. These don't need to be fancy, but they do need to be enough to represent everything your players need to know. Think about all the information to be represented in your game and make sure you have the minimum number of components required to represent it all.

QUESTIONS

Having a set of questions in mind before your playtest session will help focus feedback and should be tailored to the core concepts you are testing. You don't need a formal questionnaire, but you do need to know what questions you are trying to answer in this test cycle.

Think of the prototype as the experiment a scientist runs. What is the hypothesis this experiment is testing?

Building your first prototype is scary. It's the first time you take what is purely an idea and prepare to show it to others. Below, I will highlight some principles to demystify the process. The life of a game designer is one of constant prototyping and revising. Push yourself to get through the first few prototypes; it will get much easier over time.

KEY PRINCIPLES OF PROTOTYPING

Principle 1: Your first prototype is going to suck.

"The best is the enemy of the good."

— Voltaire

This first principle is hard for people to accept, but once you do, your life is going to get a lot easier. *Trying to make a "perfect" first prototype is a surefire recipe for never completing your game.*

Suppressing perfectionism is key to any successful creative project. To make a compelling game, you have to be willing to try new ideas and accept that many of them won't work. Only through revision of these ideas will greatness emerge. Many people get into game design because they have games they admire that they want to emulate. The quality of your prototypes should not be held to the standards of the top games you play! *Over time, your prototypes will get better, but only if you are willing to create, test, and refine them.*

Similarly, don't make the mistake of getting discouraged because players don't like your prototype or your assumptions didn't pan out. *Learning lessons cheaply is the name of the game.* Even the greatest game designers I know still make crappy first prototypes. You are in good company!

Principle 2: Be lazy.

> "Everything should be made as simple as possible,
> but not simpler."

> **— Albert Einstein**

Creating a prototype for your game is a lot of work. Whether doing a paper prototype or a digital one, a lot of time and effort will go into creating an experience that you know is going to be terrible (see Principle 1). This reality can become discouraging fast. To help make this knowledge less painful, do less work!

If you are making a card game, can you test the basic principles with a normal deck of cards (perhaps with some marker written on it)? If testing a first-person shooter, could you modify a current game to simulate the unique core concept you are trying to test? Even better, could you simulate it via a board game?

Keep in mind that you don't have to prototype a whole game to test a core concept. Playing five minutes of an experience can teach you as much as playing a forty-five-minute game if you focus on the right elements, and that extra time can be used to test out more iterations. Remember, *the goal of early prototyping is to test your core mechanic and then move quickly to the next iteration.*

Principle 3: Find the right audience.

Initial prototypes lack the polish of a finished game. Nice artwork and balanced mechanics are important parts of a final product, but they have no place in your first prototypes.

A great early playtest group is able to look past the prototype's clunkiness to see the core mechanics underneath. For this reason, other game designers are a perfect audience. Find a local game design meetup or make connections at your friendly local game store to help build a playtest group. If you don't have a sophisticated audience, you will often need to spend more time on the prototype in order to get your audience to experience the parts of the game you want to test without distraction.

The easiest games to make are those you and your friends like to play, and I highly recommend that if you are new to game design, you start with those kinds of games. Starting with games intended for your social group will make for easy-to-find audiences, and then it will be more obvious when things aren't working. If you are making games for other demographics (e.g., small children), then you will have to put in effort to find those audiences in order to get the most useful feedback.

Principle 4: Play through a whole game in your mind first.

Before finalizing your prototype, do a mental walk-through of the game. Very often when we think of ideas, we don't follow through on key details. Mentally put yourself in the player's position as he plays the game. Ask yourself refining questions during this imaginary game like:

- What do you see?

- What are your immediate incentives?

- How are you keeping track of relevant information?

A simple mental play through of a game can reveal problems before subjecting yourself to the harsh criticism of outside observers.

Principle 5: Have flexible tools.

The easier it is to make modifications to your prototype, the less resistance you will have walking through the iterative cycle. Prototyping with cards and pieces on a board that can easily be swapped out or written on with marker is far easier than having to recode a level that doesn't work.

As you move through each iteration cycle, and thus become more and more confident in the key pieces of your design, you can invest in more detailed, harder-to-change prototypes (and thus reach out to wider audiences for feedback).

PROTOTYPING TOOLS

Everyone I know has a different favorite set of prototyping tools, so experiment to find the ones that work best for you. Here are six useful ideas to get you started.

1. Physical Games and Toys

Your first goal should be to use tools that already exist. Only build something yourself if you absolutely have to. Keep a war chest of game supplies. I keep the following around at all times for playing with new ideas:

- Multiple decks of playing cards
- An *Uno* deck
- A *Go* board
- A variety of classic board games (*Monopoly*, *Scrabble*, etc.)
- Dice of all shapes and sizes
- Glass beads
- Poker chips

- A hex board with some movable tiles (e.g., *Memoir '44*, the *World of Warcraft Miniatures Game*)

- Small figurines of a variety of shapes and sizes (chess pieces work well for this, but I prefer more exotic miniatures)

- Pens, markers, and Sharpies of a variety of colors

- Large pieces of paper

- Post-it notes

- Protective card sleeves

2. Graphics Programs

If you have any skill with graphics programs, they can be a huge asset in prototyping. Adobe Photoshop and InDesign are both great for making cards if you know how to use them. If you don't know how to use them, there are free tutorials online to help you learn.

3. Simple Word Templates

If you don't have any graphics skills (I don't), you can use a Word doc template like this one (www.class-templates. com/vocabulary-flash-cards.html) for cards. Just add in text and freely available graphics as needed to get going.

4. Card Game Creators

Many programs have been designed specifically for mocking up and printing out cards. I've added a list of useful programs at thinklikeagamedesigner.com/media.

5. Digital Game Creators

During early stages, I advocate making paper prototypes if you can, but sometimes digital is the only way to go. Even if you don't have programming skills, the below tools make it relatively easy to build simple mockups.

For 2-D Game Mockups, check out Game Maker Studio.

For 3-D Game Mockups, I recommend Unity.

Again, many useful tutorials are available online if you want to brush up on your programming skills.

6. Print-on-Demand Services

Many print-on-demand services are also available for making pretty versions of your prototypes. Don't use them for your early prototypes, but they can be useful for later iterations. I use DriveThruCards.com.

EXERCISE

Go make something!

You now have all the tools necessary to make your own game! Don't get hung up on making "the perfect prototype" or finding "the perfect tool." Just get a prototype made as fast as possible and worry about improving it later. Once your prototype is complete, you are ready to put your game in front of actual players!

CHAPTER 9

Testing

"Testing leads to failure, and failure leads to understanding."

— Burt Rutan

Testing your early game prototypes is simultaneously one of the most exciting and most terrifying parts of being a designer. An inherent vulnerability comes from taking your creation and opening it up to others' criticism.

To get the most out of your testing sessions, you must learn to love criticism.

LOSE YOUR EGO

Your design is a personal creation and an extension of yourself. You were inspired by a great idea. You spent the time to set parameters, brainstorm, and prototype a game because you believe in your vision.

A part of you *knows* your design is genius, and when you show it to others, they will, without a doubt, give you some kind of award and attempt to buy your game on the spot. *Your design is your baby, and you love it unconditionally.*

This chapter is about learning to kill your babies.

The first time I was selected to lead-design a large project was for the DC Comics *Infinite Crisis* trading card game. I was so excited finally to be the lead on a big game project! I had so many cool ideas and wanted to fit them all in so this game would be the best release ever! Soon I had an entire team playing the set and seeing all the clever interactions I had baked into the design. Sometimes, the playtest group didn't fully understand the vision or see all the intricacies, but that didn't slow me down. The group would suggest I cut a few mechanics and simplify some of the designs, but I rarely heeded their advice. I knew I had a winner on my hands!

As you can probably guess, I was dead wrong but too stubborn to see it. I look back on that game now with a mixture of nostalgia and regret. I am proud of some of its elements, but all the excess clutter hid the best parts of the design, and the complexity turned off many players. My attachment to my own ideas blinded me from seeing the truth and making the best game I could.

Every game can be improved. There is always another variant that can be tested, a component that can be tweaked, or a strategy that can be better developed. I have many games I've published (even popular ones) that now make me cringe, but at the time, I thought they were the bee's knees.

Humility comes with experience. Most professional game designers learn this lesson more times than they care to admit. *Go into your testing session with the certain knowledge that your game is flawed, and embrace the opportunity to improve.* This kind of humility is not the kind that says "I can't do this," or "It's not good enough." Being creative means you have to overcome those voices in your head. The kind of humility that welcomes criticism and supports your growth as a designer is the kind that says "I will improve" and "This can get better."

The secret to loving criticism is to remove your ego from the equation. Imagine when testing a game that you are not the designer at all. In fact, you are not even friends with the designer. Furthermore, you are pretty sure the designer is an alien creature who is only just now trying to understand the human concept of "games."

Feedback from testing is not about you; it is about helping educate this alien designer. *By removing your attachment to the game being "good" or "bad," you can be far more effective at taking in and processing the reality in front of you.*

OBSERVE CLOSELY

When testing a game, keep in mind the core mechanic you are trying to test. Watch players interact with that mechanic and observe as much detail as you can. *You can elicit feedback from your players, but there is no substitute for your own observations.*

Players will often be more kind in their reviews than they would be if they didn't know you. In addition, they will often complain about things that aren't a part of the core mechanic you are trying to test. If you are testing the basics of a collectible card game resource mechanic, then don't worry about the exact numbers on the cards or complaints that your game isn't balanced. But do worry if players get confused about how the resource system works or they find themselves unable to follow the game's progress. Here are some things to look for:

- Facial expressions

- Mistaken actions

- Uncertainty of movement

- Eye movement and focus

- Strong emotional reactions

Become a keen observer of people. Do your best to allow players to make "mistakes" by doing what feels natural to them. *When in doubt, the correct action in a game should almost always be the one players naturally gravitate toward.*

As an example, in my deckbuilding game, *Ascension*, we originally had a mechanic that would remove a card from the center row each turn.

The center row moved like a conveyor belt with a new card showing up on one side and "pushing" all the other cards down the line, eliminating the last card in the row. I had a bunch of designs that manipulated the functioning of this conveyor belt. This manipulation created a lot of interesting decisions for players since the cards closest to the end of the conveyor belt would disappear if not acquired.

I found in playtesting, however, that players regularly forgot to move the conveyor belt, and I noticed it was fairly awkward to move all the cards physically with each turn. Though many players said they liked the mechanic, I decided, based on my implicit observations, to remove it, and the game improved dramatically.

ASK QUESTIONS

After a playtest session, it can sometimes be helpful to have your players fill out questionnaires to give feedback. It will depend on your audience, but you can often elicit more detailed and honest feedback with a questionnaire. Some key questions include:

- What three things did you like most about the game?

- What three things did you like least about the game?

- In your own words, what would you say this game was about?

- Was there anything you found confusing?

- If you could change one thing about the game, what would you change?

- If you could preserve one element of the game, what would you preserve?

In later phases, you can ask more general questions about the game (these aren't as useful in early stages). Examples include:

- On a scale of 1-5, how likely are you to recommend this game to a friend?

- On a scale of 1-5, how easy was this game to learn?

- On a scale of 1-5, how did you feel about the game's theme?

- On a scale of 1-5, how did you feel about the game's length?

- On a scale of 1-5, how did you feel about the game's depth of strategy?

I've created a printable version of this questionnaire for you to download and print free at thinklikeagamedesigner.com/media.

Whether you use a questionnaire or just receive direct feedback from your players, remember that the most important feedback is often unspoken. *Players don't always know what they want, and they will often identify the wrong issues as problems.*

This is not to say that you, as the designer, "know better" than your players. Your job as a designer is to engineer an experience through your game. In a fundamental way, *player perception is reality.* The key distinction is that players often don't know what will really make them feel a certain way. For example, players of collectible card games will often complain about "randomness" or "variance" ruining games when, in reality, some amount of variance is critical to making those games fun.

"When your reader tells you there is something wrong, they are almost always right. When they tell you how to fix it, they are almost always wrong."

— Neil Gaiman

Your players are the ultimate arbiters of whether your game is fun or not. The skill of a designer is discovering the specific mechanics that engineer the player experience you want. *You will refine your skills of observation as you look behind the things players say and address the way the game makes players feel.* When possible, run your playtest session with a few different groups to get a wider range of feedback. Sometimes, one player's reaction can be dismissed, but recurring comments from players in your target demographic are almost always something that needs to be addressed.

EXERCISE

Test your prototype!

Schedule a playtest session for your prototype. Watch for both implicit and explicit feedback and jot down your notes from the session.

If you've come this far, congratulations! This is the nuts and bolts of being a game designer. The final step is to take what you've learned and use that information to iterate on the process again. We will cover that in the next chapter.

CHAPTER 10

Iterating

"Success is going from failure to failure
without loss of enthusiasm."

— Winston Churchill

Once you've gotten feedback from testing your game, the next step is to evaluate that feedback and use it to repeat the core design loop cycle.

Your primary goal in each core design loop cycle is to test your core concept against the realities of an actual session of play. Keep your ego out of the equation and look honestly at the data you received from your playtest session. When looking at the data, there are three possible results:

1. Your core concept works.
2. Your core concept doesn't work.
3. Your core concept sorta worked, maybe?

Let's look at each result in detail.

YOUR CORE CONCEPT WORKS

You tested your idea and got a great response. This is awesome news! Even if your design has significant flaws (it almost certainly does), you got enough positive feedback on the core concept you were testing to want to move forward. Before going too far forward, however, I recommend testing your game with at least one other group to make sure the first test group wasn't biased in your favor (my mom loves all my games, even if she doesn't understand how to play). *The best test for knowing whether players liked your game is if they ask to play again.*

Now you should begin asking more detailed questions about how to best highlight and support this core concept. What new theory will you test with the next iteration? Some good questions to ask are:

- What was more fun than I thought it would be?
- What got in the way of the fun?
- What else can I do to support the core mechanic?

With these questions answered, do a quick review of your inspiration list and framing. Then, scan your brainstorm list for ideas that can serve as the next core concept to test. Add ideas that come to you after the playtest session. Then, prototype again and schedule another test session. Continue to refine your core mechanic until it really shines.

YOUR CORE CONCEPT DOESN'T WORK

If your playtest didn't go as well as you had hoped, this is also great news! I know what you are thinking: *How can it be great news that my idea didn't work?* It's great news because *criticism is the lifeblood of the creative process.*

This concrete feedback is exactly the kind of criticism you learn to love because it provides valuable information on how to move forward. The key is to take the lessons and use them to inform your next iteration.

Ask yourself these key questions:

- Why didn't the core concept work out as planned?

- Was there something I didn't foresee that could be changed or removed?

- Was there something about this prototype that people enjoyed more than I expected?

Maybe a new idea was spawned from the session that you can work on for the next round. You can also go back to your brainstorm notes to see whether other ideas can serve as a focus for the next design.

Sometimes, you need to go back for more inspiration before making another prototype. Don't let an initial lack of success dissuade you! *There are many paths forward. Your job as a designer is to keep moving until you find the right path for you and your players.*

YOUR CORE CONCEPT SORTA WORKED, MAYBE?

Far worse than concrete negative feedback is mixed, wishy-washy feedback. If you receive mixed feedback, it makes it hard to know how to proceed.

Uncertainty is the hardest situation to handle; unfortunately, it is a very common one. Often, your playtest session is neither a roaring success nor a complete disaster.

Perhaps the feedback was mixed on your core concept. Perhaps other issues (like an insufficient prototype or inappropriate audience) muddied the results you were looking for. The challenge here is that the specific path forward is unclear. You don't know what to try next. This is dangerous territory for a designer since many games become orphaned designs and end up on a shelf without a plan to revive them.

Finding that clear path forward is challenging, but in general, there are two approaches to use:

1. TRY AGAIN

If you don't feel like your core concept got a fair shake, try with a different playgroup or a more refined prototype to see whether you get clear results. Maybe a small tweak to the core concept will solve your problem, or maybe the core idea is better expressed in a different way.

Go back through the steps of the core design loop and give it another shot with your best guess at what revisions might help.

2. LET IT SIT

Sometimes, the right thing to do is put a design down and start working on something else. First, make sure all of your game rules, parameters, core concept, and brainstorm ideas are written down and organized somewhere so they can be picked up again. While in the middle of a design process, you have everything in your head, so it's easy to make small adjustments and see the bigger picture. After taking a break from a design, you'll be surprised how much you forget. I've lost countless designs because I forgot to write things down in detail. Don't let this happen to you! Hunan Beef!

Set a calendar reminder for yourself to come back to the game in a few weeks. Often, returning with fresh eyes can help you see the big picture more clearly.

THE PATH FORWARD

"It always seems impossible until it's done."

— Nelson Mandela

Work your way through the steps of the core design loop until you reach a game you are happy with. Each time you go through the core design loop, you will refine the questions you ask. I refer to this concept as the "phases of design," and it is covered in the upcoming chapters.

If your concept is working, increasingly move through the design phases to refine your product. If something isn't working, circle back to revise and iterate until you find a solution. *Keep momentum and enthusiasm going! If you've gone through this entire cycle more than once, you are living the life of a game designer!*

PART III

Refining Your Designs

. . . .

CHAPTER 11

The Phases of Design

"Efficiency, which is doing things right, is irrelevant
until you work on the right things."

— Peter Drucker

We've now gone through all the steps of the core design loop, which is the fundamental building block for designing games. This loop, however, forms the foundation of a much larger process that brings you from the beginning of your design all the way to a finished product. The five phases of design below outline how you shift focus during your design iterations, allowing you to zero in on what is important in each phase.

Each phase layers on top of another with the core design loop supporting each.

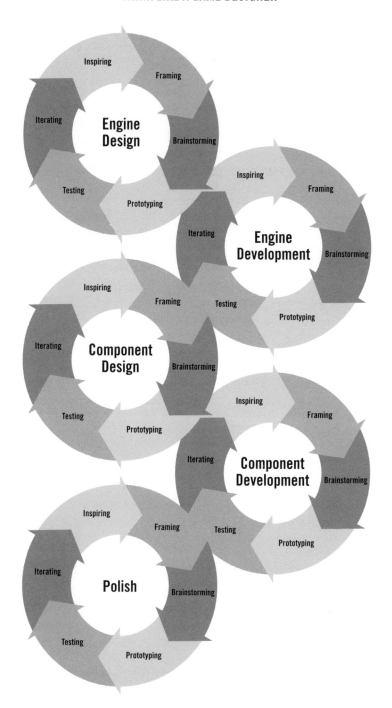

Building a game is a lot like building a house. You need to build things in the proper order and with the proper emphasis to make a game that will stand the test of time. Imagine trying to build a house by first arranging furniture on an empty lot. As you might guess, this is a recipe for disaster. Since there are no rooms built yet, it really doesn't matter how great a job you do selecting and placing your sofa!

While the process of design isn't complicated, *if you do things in the wrong order, you will find a lot of your work ends up wasted* and needing to be redone. Many designers I speak to spend a lot of time worrying about the metaphorical paint color while their design's foundation is still unsound. Don't fall into this trap!

Before we get too deep into analyzing each of the phases of design, here are two rules to keep in mind:

Rule #1: Design Phases Are Fluid

Usually, no hard line exists between when you should work on one phase or another. You can't, for example, properly test a game engine without at least some defined components. Similarly, you will often discover engine improvements while working on component development. Each phase shifts the emphasis of your testing, not the essential nature of the process.

Rule #2: The Core Design Loop Is Still King

The core design loop is at the foundation of all good design. Each of the five phases represents a different focus as you go through the core design loop. You should expect to complete at least one loop during each phase (most likely far more than one).

Hopefully, by now, you've done the exercises in previous chapters and practiced at least one iteration of the core design loop. Master the core design loop before worrying too much about the design phases.

THE FIVE PHASES OVERVIEW

The process of game design can be broken down into five phases.

1.   Engine Design
2.   Engine Development
3.   Component Design
4.   Component Development
5.   Polish

Each of the five phases has different questions that serve as the focus of your testing. *Equally important are the questions you should not answer in each phase.* A common mistake among game designers is getting distracted by questions that aren't relevant yet. The five phases help to keep your focus where it needs to be.

Let's look at an overview of each of the design phases. We will dig deeper in the following chapters.

ENGINE DESIGN

The engine is the foundation of your game "house." At this phase, your main purpose is to take your core inspiration and find out how it will be expressed in your game. I call this Engine Design because it is what makes the whole game run at a deep level, just like the engine in a car. This is the period when you take your big ideas and turn them into testable realities. Don't get bogged down in minutiae during this phase. Look past the superficial and focus on fundamentals. Key questions are:

- What is the core game loop?
- What is the game's fundamental tension?
- How do players interact?
- What is the game's main resource?
- What is the game's objective?
- Why is this game fun?

ENGINE DEVELOPMENT

During Engine Development, you are finishing your game's basic framework. Now is when you shape your game design house with walls and a roof. At this point, your core game loop should be clearly defined as additional rules are added, tweaked, and removed to hit your objectives. Key questions are:

- What is the average game length?
- How are game elements represented?
- How many components are required?
- What are the approximate number ranges used in the game?
- What are the exchange rates between different game resources?

COMPONENT DESIGN

Component Design is where you decide what goes into your house, picking out the accessories, curtains, and appliances. The focus is on making sure the different pieces of each room fit your purposes and make sense together. Here is where you begin to flesh out all of the elements of your game, be they cards, figures, loot drops, or anything else.

When doing initial component design for collectible or expandable games, it's important to build systems that support the player in understanding the dozens, hundreds, or thousands of collectible objects you will create over time. These systems give players the ability to process all this information by "chunking" the objects into larger groups. To do this, you need to ask:

- How am I "chunking" components into categories?

- What themes will be prominent in the game?

- What structures help players understand what is happening?

- What play patterns do I want to highlight?

COMPONENT DEVELOPMENT

Component Development is where your game design house becomes livable; you place all the furniture exactly where you want it. This is where you focus on the strength of different strategies and ensure that players are incentivized to do the things you want them to do. Most designers place too much emphasis on this phase too early, but now is the time to ask:

- How balanced are the available strategies?

- Are there answers to degenerate strategies?

- Are the fun play patterns emphasized?

POLISH

Polish is the final layer of paint and decoration to make your game design house beautiful. It is what separates professional games from amateur prototypes. As great as your game may be, if it doesn't look good and make sense to the consumer, it will never succeed. Here is where you can let your inner obsessive compulsive disorder run rampant. During this phase, the focus is on:

- Customer Facing Rules and Tutorials
- Templating and User Interface
- Art, Names, Story

Those are the basics of each design phase! Each phase is designed with specific questions in mind to guide your core design loop and make sure you aren't spending too much time on things that don't matter yet. Don't worry if everything isn't clear; the following chapters will dig deeper into how to manage each phase.

CHAPTER 12

Engine Design

"Creativity is always a leap of faith. You're faced with a blank page, blank easel, or an empty stage."

— James Cameron

For many writers, the blank page is the scariest part of the job. Engine Design is the blank page for building games, and it can be intimidating to try to build a system with so many moving parts. But don't let the open-ended nature of this phase intimidate you!

Your goal is to answer a few key questions to help give shape to your game. You will have plenty of time later to work out details and refine your concept. Stay focused on these big picture questions to get your core engine running. In this chapter, we will review the questions and look at the types of answers you might select.

1. WHAT IS THE CORE GAME LOOP?

A core game loop is the basic pattern of play at the heart of your game. *The core game loop should almost always be de-*

scribable in a sentence or two. In *Go,* the core game loop is placing stones one at a time and trying to capture territory. In *Call of Duty,* the core game loop is getting weapons and ammo, looking for enemies, and killing enemies before they kill you.

You will need to have other elements defined to test the core game loop properly (e.g., how does a player move, what are the damage ranges of various weapons, how high can my character jump, etc.), but these elements should be loosely defined and flexible. The goal is for all the peripheral rules and elements to be only "good enough" to test the core game loop. You will have time to improve all the peripherals later.

There will be many broken things about your game in this phase. Strategies are not balanced, pieces are ugly, and many fundamental elements are still in flux. A designer has to look through all of that to see whether there is a diamond of fun in the rough prototype. Training your instincts to find the fun and ignore the rough patches in early testing is critical.

While working on our digital collectible game *SolForge,* we had to do all of our initial prototyping on paper while still trying to design a game that worked best in digital. This required a lot of ugly hacks to make the game work. A single game could take well over two hours to set up and play. After that, we would usually change many things that could take several more hours to update and set up.

After going through multiple failed systems, including some that contained terrain, fog of war, NPC (non-player character) monsters, and more, we settled on the basic core loop of cards that level up as you play them.

When you have a basic core game loop that is fun, you are ready to move on to the next phase.

2. WHAT IS THE GAME'S FUNDAMENTAL TENSION?

Your job as a game designer is to frustrate your players. I know that sounds strange, but hear me out. Every game gives players a goal and then puts roadblocks in their way. Your goal in chess, for example, is to capture the opponent's king, but the game wouldn't be any fun if you could just reach across the table and grab it!

Good game design puts restrictions on how you are allowed to act. This makes the goal challenging to reach. The "fun" of gameplay is the process of navigating through obstacles to move toward your objective. Be conscious of what these tensions are. In many ways, this fundamental tension is what your game is really about.

In the tile-laying game *Carcassone*, players alternate placing tiles and tokens to claim territory and score points for finishing roads, castles, and other structures. The game's tension comes from having access to only one tile each turn. Finding the right tiles to finish your structures while tactically using tile placement to protect yourself or make things more difficult for your opponents is the heart of the game.

In *SolForge*, the fundamental tension is around the core leveling system. Since each card levels when you play it, you need to consider both the current effect and the leveled card's future impact. Players must decide whether to play cards that are good right now but don't level as well versus cards that are weaker now but are strong in the late game. This decision, in turn, informs the opponent's decision about which cards to play.

Almost all games have multiple layers of tension, not just one. For example, *Carcassone* has a limited number of tokens you can use to claim territory, so deciding when to use and when to hold back tokens is a key tension. *SolForge* also has lane-based combat, creating a tension of whether to place your creatures defensively to stop opposing creatures or offensively in empty lanes. In *Monopoly*, you need to balance spending money for property and houses against retaining enough funds to pay rent when you need to. Tension also exists around a limited number of houses being available, which can restrict your ability to build if you fall behind.

It is valuable to identify all the tensions in your game, but *it is critical to identify the fundamental tension.* Whenever making decisions about your game, always ask, "Does this reinforce or weaken the fundamental tension of this game?" If a mechanic removes focus from the fundamental tension, remove it.

Many hard-to-answer questions arise throughout the game design process. Identifying the fundamental tension early in the process will help guide you in answering those questions.

3. WHAT ARE YOUR GAME'S RESOURCES?

Games are about using resources to interact with the system and achieve a goal. These terms can be very loosely defined, but you do need to define each to make your game work. What resources does the player have access to (e.g., cards, gold, action points, a thirty-minute timer, etc.)? Most games have more than one resource, and it is the interaction between those limited resources that creates the tension of play. The types of resources you choose to include have a dramatic effect on the feelings evoked and the complexity of learning the game.

TYPES OF RESOURCES

1. Scaling

Scaling resources start off small at the game's beginning but become more plentiful as the game progresses. These resources replenish every turn regardless of whether or not they are used. I use the term "turn" here, but it applies equally well to real-time games. Depending on the game's speed, a certain amount of elapsed time counts as a turn.

Examples of scaling resources include playing one land per turn in *Magic*, or gaining one energy per turn in *Hearthstone*. Pretty much every RPG has a scaling resource represented in new and improved abilities gained while leveling up.

Scaling resources have the advantage of creating a sense of progression throughout the game. Small effects are relevant in the early game, with bigger effects showing up later. This sense of progress is psychologically rewarding and the tension of choosing to focus on late game versus early game often creates a depth of strategy.

2. Fixed

Fixed resources don't change throughout the game. A fixed resource must either be spent or it will be lost and reset the following turn. Most classic games have a fixed resource of taking one action per turn (e.g., moving a piece in chess, rolling the dice in *Monopoly*, etc.). Turn-based strategy games like *Civilization* have a fixed resource of commanding each unit once per turn, and most miniatures games have figures in play that all get to move and act once each turn.

Fixed resources have the advantage of being simple and easy to understand. Because of this simplicity, the fixed resource is the fundamental building block of most games. When using fixed resources, however, you need to find other ways to create a sense of progression.

3. Accumulating

Accumulating resources are those that store up from turn to turn if you don't spend them. Any card game where you draw a fixed number of cards each turn has an accumulating resource. The accumulating elixir in Supercell's *Clash Royale* and the gold in *World of Warcraft* are other examples of accumulating resources.

Since accumulating resources are not lost if unspent, there is less pressure on each turn to spend them. Player decisions involving accumulating resources tend to be very complicated since players must evaluate spending a resource not just in the context of this turn, but also for all possible future turns.

One way to combat the complexity of an accumulating resource is to put a restriction on how many resources can be kept from turn to turn (e.g., a maximum hand limit or mana limit). The smaller the maximum relative to the resources accumulated each turn, the closer this gets to a fixed resource.

4. WHAT ARE THE AXES OF INTERACTION IN YOUR GAME?

Interaction is what distinguishes games from other creative media. Your engine needs to have defined ways to interact—whether that is with the game system (in a single player game) or with other players. The types of interaction you select are probably the most important factor for the overall "feel" of your game engine.

TYPES OF INTERACTION

1. Shared Resources

A shared resource is any limited resource that multiple players have access to. In my deckbuilding game *Ascension*, most of the interaction takes place in the center row of cards. Players try to get the best cards for themselves, while denying key cards to their opponents. In the real-time strategy game *StarCraft*, key resources used to create more units are located around the map that players battle to control.

I find it useful to subdivide further the shared resources into "hot" and "cold" shared resources.

Hot shared resources are those that make it very clear when a player can take something from another player. Hot shared resources are prevalent in territory control games like *Settlers of Catan*, *StarCraft*, and *Ticket to Ride*. Hot shared resources create more tension and excitement, but they can also lead to anxiety and hostility when players visibly lose out on resources they really want.

Cold shared resources are more subtle. Players drafting cards from hidden packs and then passing them to other players are still taking resources from each other, but the hidden nature of the selection removes some of the tension and emotional charge from the decision. Even as small a distinction as shifting from taking spaces on a map to taking from a shared pool of cards can have a dramatic impact on the game's feeling, even if the abstract mechanics are the same.

2. Direct Attack

Direct attacking games are those where players attempt to attack or destroy opposing players' resources. Examples are attacking a player's life total in *Magic: The Gathering*, shooting players in *Call of Duty*, or capturing pieces in a game of chess. Direct attacking makes a game feel deeply interactive. Each success from my side will be felt as a loss to my opponent. *The biggest challenge in direct attacking games is a runaway leader advantage.* This occurs if the resource being attacked is critical to playing the game. Attacking a player's life total in *Magic* doesn't have this problem (typically) because life total is not used to play the game. Attacking another player's creatures or cards in hand, however, does tend to create this kind of negative tension. Being careful when direct attacking critical game resources is a primary feature of your game.

3. Deduction

Deduction games require you to assess the other players (social deduction) or clues from the game itself (puzzle deduction) for information. Examples of social deduction include *Apples to Apples*, poker, and *Pictionary*. Examples of puzzle deduction include crosswords, Sudoku, and Escape Rooms.

Social deduction games interact on a psychological level, where getting to know the other players is key to playing well. They trigger our need to understand other people. Social deduction mechanics can create deep gameplay without a lot of complex rules. The key to setting up good deduction interactions is to *structure the game so each player reveals bits and pieces of information over time, thus forcing the other players to fill in the gaps and get the information they want.*

Puzzle games derive enjoyment from the tension and release of figuring things out. If a puzzle is too hard, the player only experiences frustration. If a puzzle is too easy, there is no satisfaction in figuring out the solution. Puzzle games, thus, need to be very targeted to the right difficulty level for the players. Having a variety of difficulty modes and/or unlockable hints to help players move along at an appropriate pace are key to keeping the puzzle experience fun for a wide audience.

5. HOW DOES YOUR GAME END?

While not every game has a "winner," most games have some condition that players are trying to achieve, and all games need some mechanism for ending. *As a game designer, victory is the carrot at the end of the stick that you are using to lead players to a fun experience.* The specifics of your victory condition are probably the least important of the engine level questions, but differences in how you structure your end-game conditions will have subtle ripple effects throughout your game.

TYPES OF END-GAME CONDITIONS

1. Player Elimination

The most obvious victory condition is the removal of all other players from the game. This is easy to understand and a solid choice for any two-player game. In multiplayer games, however, be careful about eliminating players too early because forcing people to sit around and watch others play can be a drag. Games like *Magic: The Gathering* and *Warhammer* utilize this type of victory condition.

2. Time Limit

The game lasts a certain amount of time based on either an explicit timer or an implicit depleting resource. At the end of the allotted time, whoever has done the best according to some key metric is then declared the winner. Games like *Bejeweled*, *Ascension*, and *Ra* utilize this type of victory condition. Time limit games are often at their best when you get a sense that time is running short, but you don't exactly know when the game will end.

3. Goal Achieving

The game lasts until a player achieves some specific goal. This gives players a clear direction in the game, but it can often constrain your design space down the road. *Citadels*, *Settlers of Catan*, and most single player games use this type of victory condition. It is often useful to hide information about how close players are to achieving their goals until the very end. This withholding helps maintain tension and excitement even if one player is far ahead.

EXERCISE

Pick a design you are working on and answer the core engine questions for it.

What is the core play loop for your game?

_____

_____

What is the fundamental tension?

_____

_____

What are your resources?

_____

_____

What are the axes of interaction?

_____

_____

How does the game end?

_____

_____

Games can use multiple systems from each of the above categories, and there are endless permutations. Have fun experimenting and laying the groundwork for your next playtest!

CHAPTER 13

Engine Development

"There are no sure answers, only better questions."

— Dick Van Dyke

If the core engine design is laying the foundation of your game house, core engine development is the framing upon which everything else will hang. At the end of this phase, your game should be fun and meet your design goals, although it will not be balanced or polished.

Here are some key areas of focus during engine development:

1. WHAT ARE THE FUNDAMENTAL COMPONENTS?

Build the Basics

Your goal in this phase is not to design all of your game's components! You will, however, need to have at least some of your components in place to develop the engine properly. It is a common misconception that to prototype and test a game, you need to be able to complete an entire game. At these early stages, nothing could be further from the truth!

Often, a five-minute session focused on what you are trying to learn is more valuable than playing through an entire forty-five-minute game. The five-minute session allows you to prototype less and iterate more, which is the name of the game in the core design loop.

In a fighting game, have at least 3-4 characters with relatively defined traits. In a trading card game, have 2-3 pre-built decks to test with. The key is a small number of permutations that highlight a few of the strategies available in your game.

You do not need to worry about the strategies being fully fleshed out or balanced. You can include a few things that push the engine's boundaries, but for the most part, you just want nuts and bolts effects at this stage. Too many wacky components can make it harder to see what is going on at the engine level.

Define Number and Value Ranges

To define your fundamental components, you will have to set some numbers. How many components is your game going to have? What are the number ranges going to be? How long do you want a typical game to last? The key in this phase is not to get the numbers exactly right, but just to know the ballpark you want to be working in so you can test your game's assumptions.

2. WHAT ARE THE GAME RULES?

By the time you leave this phase, you should be able to write up the rules for your game (though they will change). How do units move? At what rate do players draw cards? What are the rules for line-of-sight and stun effects? How can players transfer one game resource into another?

Try out a variety of answers to these questions in this phase as you iterate. By iterating on a variety of possible complete rule sets, you can see how your fundamental components interact with those rules to make a game that is fun and not completely broken.

Write Things Down!

I cannot stress enough the importance of writing things down during this phase. Writing things down has a few advantages. Most importantly, it prevents you from forgetting the work you've done.

Written rules also make collaboration with other designers and playtesters much easier. The sooner you can get people testing your game from written rules, the better your rules will be at the end of the process.

Old written-down rules are also a great tool for writing design articles and talking about your process after the game's release. Writing down rules early makes everything better in the long run. If you take one lesson from this book, make it this one.

Use Rejected Rules to Aid Later Design

Almost every rejected rule during your iteration process can assist you in your design down the road. Collectible game design, in particular, is all about using your components to break the engine rules. In my digital game *SolForge*, for example, creatures you played originally only attacked during your turn. For a variety of reasons, the game ended up working better when all creatures attacked on both players' turns. However, we designed multiple cards that don't attack during the opponent's turn because we knew the advantages of that system from earlier testing.

3. WHAT ARE PLAYERS INCENTIVIZED TO DO?

Fundamentally, what does the player want to do when playing your game? What behaviors does the core game loop encourage? If players are systemically avoiding interacting with each other in a board game, your core loop may have a problem. Game incentives should generally reward people for doing things that are natural and fun, with more layers of options being revealed over time. Watch player behavior and see how your core game loop pushes them to behave.

Make Player Instincts Correct

Try and make a player's natural instincts be (most of the time) the correct thing to do. If your players are constantly taking a certain course of action, embrace it.

In my deckbuilding game *Ascension*, most casual players focused almost exclusively on attacking monsters. The original game engine made that almost a surefire losing strategy against players who first acquired cards to improve their decks.

After many playtest sessions, I rebalanced the engine to make an early monster attack strategy viable. This rebalancing took a long time to figure out because my personal instinct was always to improve my deck first and then defeat monsters. Keep an eye out for when your personal play style doesn't match that of your average player.

Times Two or Divide By Two

When working with numbers in your game at this stage, it is best to move in big chunks, not small increments. When in doubt, double the number or cut it in half. Since developing a game engine requires you to set your number ranges, experiment in big chunks to learn faster. If a system is not working right, try doubling the numbers to push the mechanic or cut numbers in half to reduce the importance.

These new numbers won't be exactly right, but they will inform you if you are moving in the right direction more quickly than making many subtle changes along the way (there is time for that later). *SolForge* creatures were originally on a much smaller scale than they are now, but we found that the creatures all felt too similar. When we doubled the range of numbers for attack and defense (and quadrupled player health), it gave us far more room to design cards that felt different from each other. Experiment with radical shifts to help shake things up and break your preconceived notions of how the game "should" go.

4. IS THIS FUN?

It is easy to get lost in the minutiae of mechanics, but *player experience is the only metric that matters*. Does the game evoke the feelings you are generally looking for? Is the game length approximately where you want it to be? Are you staying true to your initial vision, or has your vision changed?

Ideally, when you leave this phase, your game's fundamentals are relatively stable. If you aren't happy with the feel of the game (knowing that things like balance and polish are still to come), now is the time to try to fix any issues that arise. You can shore up problems with good component design and development, but the engine level decisions will have long-reaching impacts for your game's life, so take the time to get this part right.

CHAPTER 14

Component Design

"Design is not just what it looks like and feels like.
Design is how it works."

— Steve Jobs

Component design is where you fill in the pieces that finally make a game playable to completion by a more general audience. With very few exceptions, most modern games have many individual components that all need to work together to bring the game to life. Whether your game components are cards, weapons, characters, spells, or all of the above, the same principles apply to make these disparate elements work together.

When working on engine design and development, you have to design the minimum number of components required to test the engine. Now, you need to flesh out the rest of your game. Building out all the components of your game is a daunting task, particularly if you are designing a digital or collectible game with hundreds (or thousands) of components. The way to overcome this complexity is through structure.

Successful component design is all about creating structure so everything has a proper place. By having a structure in your mind, components already in your head will have natural homes and you will notice the gaps in each part of your structure that will suggest needed designs. In addition to helping you during your design process, having structure will help your players process new information as they learn your game. I discuss this concept in more detail in Chapter 18: Elegance.

A pervasive myth is that creativity is about being free from constraint. The opposite is true. Creativity can only thrive in a world with a solid structure upon which the creative impulse can be unleashed. How you build that structure is the key to good component design.

CATEGORIES

At the highest level, you need to break down your components into categories. Examples of categories are:

- Colors in *Magic: The Gathering*
- Classes in *World of Warcraft*
- Roles in *League of Legends*
- Weapons in *Destiny*
- Property types in *Monopoly*

Categories are defined by theme as well as mechanical function. The easiest way to define them is to answer questions about the extremes. The more complex your game, the more questions you will need to answer.

Mechanical Questions

1. What does this category do mechanically?
2. What is this category best at?
3. What is this category worst at?

Thematic Questions

1. What does this category represent?
2. What does this category care about or want the most?
3. What does this category hate or fear the most?

By answering these questions, you will begin to get a feel for what belongs in a category and what doesn't. You will inevitably flesh out more details over time, but the big picture questions above are enough to get started.

In *Magic: The Gathering*, cards are broken down into colors. Each color has a theme (e.g., red is about fire, passion, and living in the moment). Each color has mechanical strengths (e.g., red is the best at doing damage quickly) and mechanical weaknesses (e.g., red cannot destroy enchantments and has few flying creatures). By knowing the category's details, it is both easier for a designer to make cards that belong in a color as well as for players to understand why they might want (or not want) to have red cards in their deck.

In games like *World of Warcraft*, you must select a class to begin the game. Each class has a strictly defined set of abilities and advancement trees. *Warriors*, for example, can take a lot of damage and work best at close range. Each class determines which items you will be able to use and the role you will play in raids. Roles include Tanks (designed to absorb damage and protect other players), Healers, and DPS (designed to maximize "damage per second" to take out enemies quickly). These roles, while not formally presented in the game, represent even higher level categories that each class falls into, and they further help to divide and understand new classes as they are introduced.

SUBCATEGORIES

Subcategories (aka subtypes, subthemes) give you more ways to divide your components. Think of your categories as the Russian nesting dolls of structure. Each layer can contain within it increasingly refined levels of detail. Once you have defined the top level, repeat the same process to create sub-themes within each category.

In *World of Warcraft*, Warlocks are a class of magic users who power their magic with health and sacrifice. But each talent tree has its own particular focus. Demonology Talent Warlocks generally focus on summoning strong creatures to fight for them, while Affliction Warlocks focus on putting negative effects on their enemies to hurt them over time. In *Magic's* green color, which is about growth and nature, Elves tend to provide additional resources while Beasts tend to be larger creatures intended for attacking.

CYCLES

A cycle is a single theme or pattern that repeats itself across multiple categories. You can also have cycles within a category to highlight a key feature (e.g., have a small, medium, and large version of a core effect). Cycles are one of the best ways to establish your themes and communicate them to players.

In basic games like *Monopoly*, cycles are easy to spot. When I compare the two-color set of Boardwalk and Park Place to the two-color set of Baltic and Mediterranean Avenues, I can easily understand that Boardwalk is much more expensive and valuable. Often, even in complex collectible games, the cycles jump out at you right away. One of the most famous trading card game cycles is from *Magic's* very first set. The cycle was all one-cost instants that provided three of something.

The red card, Lightning Bolt, did 3 damage. The blue card, Ancestral Recall, drew 3 cards. The black one, Dark Ritual, produced 3 mana. The white one, Healing Salve, prevented 3 damage, and the green one, Giant Growth, increased a creature's attack and toughness by 3. All the cards are united by costing 1 and providing 3 of something. From looking at the cards alone, you can instantly learn a lot about what defines each color. Some cycles are more subtle than what I described above, but each still follows the basic principle of holding something constant while using variation to highlight important traits.

Cycles are powerful because by keeping so many elements the same, you draw a player's attention to the differences. These differences reinforce your game's structure. In addition, when a player sees two or three parts of this cycle, he or she will want to look for the final pieces. This helps drive excitement as players speculate about what the final piece of the puzzle will look like.

When in doubt, add more cycles and structure. It is hard to overdo it.

BREAKING STRUCTURE

Game design is an art form, and like all rules in art, the structural rules above are meant to be broken. You will regularly encounter specific designs or sub-themes that break from your initial direction, but you shouldn't break rules until you've spent time working within them.

Breaking structure should be done with purpose to draw particular attention to a feature. For example, in *Magic*, the color green doesn't typically have any flying creatures. When a green flying dragon is introduced, however, it highlights how rare and special that creature is. Judicious use of broken structures is a powerful tool, but only if you spend effort building up those structures in the first place.

FILL IN THE SKELETON

Once you've built out your structure, you have a map of what your completed set of components should look like. At this point, I will typically break out a spreadsheet and start filling it in with designs. Create a skeleton outline with the number of components you want in each category. Then block off time and start filling in the gaps. Now that you know the structure, your creative mind will instinctively start to fill in designs, so the process for creating your first set of components should flow smoothly. The tools in Chapter 7 on Brainstorming are particularly useful here. If you get stuck, fall back on creating more cycles or try adding a new subcategory to help move you forward.

Once your components are designed, it is time to get to the development process.

CHAPTER 15

Component Development

"The details are not the details. They make the design."

— Charles Eames

During component development, attention shifts from the big picture to the small details. In this phase, you may spend hours agonizing over one additional point of power or resource cost on a component. Leading up to this phase, those issues could (and should) be overlooked in favor of focus on the bigger vision for the design. Now, it's time to get into the weeds.

My first job in the gaming industry was as a game developer for the *Vs. System* trading card game. I was recruited because of my success on the *Magic: The Gathering* Pro Tour, during which my primary focus was to find degenerate strategies and exploit them. This skill set is incredibly valuable, but it is very different from a designer's skill set. Let's define the skill sets of both roles:

- A great designer understands the player's emotional experience and can create rules and components that evoke desired emotions and experiences.

- A great developer understands the strategic implications of different rules and components and is able to balance them to support the design's emotional intent.

Both roles must support each other to create a great game.

If the designer doesn't create fun and powerful emotional experiences, the best development cannot make a good game.

If the developer completely misses the mark, then the designer's vision will never be realized.

We've talked a lot about the key elements of design, so now, let's break down how to think about developing your game by looking at three key paradigms.

DEVELOPMENT PARADIGM 1: BALANCE

Fundamentally, development is about balance. A balanced game is one in which no single strategy is so dominant that another strategy cannot defeat it.

Balance does not mean equal!

Your goal in development is not to make all components, cards, or strategies equally strong, only to make sure that no one is completely dominant. Part of the fun of playing games is finding the more powerful strategies and components. If none are more powerful, you rob the player of the joy of discovery. Don't try to make everything equal; just make sure the most powerful thing isn't so powerful that the joy of discovery is lost once that thing is found.

Silver Bullets

One valuable tool to help ensure diversity of strategies in your game is to include silver bullets. The term comes from the myth that werewolves could only be killed by silver bullets. Silver is not a great metal to make bullets from, but if you happen to have a werewolf problem on your hands, you sure will be happy you have them.

In game design, silver bullets are components that aren't necessarily good on their own, but they are devastatingly effective against some strategies. The most classic example of a balanced game is rock-paper-scissors. In this game, each choice provides a definitive answer to another player's possible strategy, so no one play can ever become dominant. In many roleplaying games, players have the option to don "Resistance to X" (e.g., Fire) armor, which they can use when facing a difficult foe of type X.

Another classic example from a more complex game is *Magic: The Gathering's Circles of Protection.*

Each circle could stop all damage from a single color. If your opponent didn't play that color, it was useless. If he played *only* that color, that one card could win you the game.

If one strategy becomes too dominant, then players can use silver bullets to defeat it. This isn't a panacea to solve all development challenges, but it can help prevent the worst-case scenario of one strategy being unbeatable. Be careful not to make your silver bullet components too powerful lest they themselves become the dominant strategy.

Use Development Knobs to Find Balance

Your core engine will dictate how easy it is to balance your game. Do your creatures all have one power number or two? Are there different types of costs or only one? I call these balance points "development knobs" because each one can be turned like a knob on a tuning board to help you find a balance point. In general, the more knobs you have, the easier it is to balance your game.

I'll discuss how game engine level systems can help development in Chapter 20: Depth.

DEVELOPMENT PARADIGM 2: STRATEGY ARCHETYPES

When creating initial components, it helps to group components into general player strategy archetypes. Note that these archetypes are different from motivation archetypes, which will be discussed in Chapter 21: Motivation.

The basic strategy archetypes are:

Defensive: The player tries to survive long enough to set up an insurmountable late game advantage.

Offensive: The player tries to win quickly, before other players can execute their strategy.

Stealth: The player tries to obfuscate his or her position and uses misinformation to gain an edge.

Combo: The player tries to combine two or more resources in a way that gives him or her an overpowering edge.

These are loose definitions since most player strategies will involve a combination of all the above. But it can be helpful to simplify them for your initial creation process. Not every game will support every strategy type, but it is worth considering how each might be reflected in your design. When developing components, think how each player's strategy archetype might execute his or her preferred strategy.

DEVELOPMENT PARADIGM 3: FUN FIRST

The unfortunate truth about component development is that you will never get it 100 percent right. I've worked with some of the most brilliant game developers in the world and spent years developing a single release. Even with all those resources, I still made mistakes.

Huge companies that spend millions of dollars and years developing their games still make development mistakes. I can guarantee that you will too. The question is: How do you handle it when you do?

The first rule is: When in doubt, push the fun. Pay attention to which play patterns are most enjoyable and which ones make players want to quit. In a trading card game, it is all right if giant dragons win a lot of games, but it's not all right if resource denial prevents one player from ever playing a card.

The second rule is: Be humble. Be prepared to admit mistakes and keep an eye out for what is changing. Games are living organisms that change both in response to new content and player behavior trends. If your game is successful, you will get opportunities to correct your mistakes (and to make new ones).

Games are compelling because players get to craft their own game experiences from the tools you give them. Learn from your players and be ready to adapt to the game you all create together.

CHAPTER 16

Polish

"Pixar has been compared to fine furniture makers who polish the backs of drawers—even if you don't see everything in a particular scene, you still feel that every little detail has been met."

— John Lasseter

If you've come this far, you've got a pretty awesome game. You've crafted your vision, defined your frame, brainstormed countless ideas, and prototyped and iterated on them repeatedly. With each phase of design, your cycles got tighter and tighter, focusing on more minutiae until the entire system hummed. Now it's time to put the final touches on your game and make it ready for the public.

THEME

Sometimes, your theme is established at the beginning of your design process. When I was designing a collectible card game for Marvel and DC characters, it was obvious that the theme would be comic book heroes and villains doing battle.

Usually, however, I build a game's mechanics before deciding on a final theme. That's not to say I don't think about theme during the entire design process; it's simply that theme isn't the main focus of the design, and thus, it doesn't get the attention it needs until the polish phase. How much time needs to be spent at this stage will depend greatly on the type of game you are making and your development budget. A board game takes less time than a collectible card game, which, in turn, takes less time than a massive multiplayer online game. Sometimes you hit on a great theme early on; other times, you may struggle to find the right fit for your game.

For an illustrative example, let's look at a light, social card game I helped design called *You Gotta Be Kitten Me*.

Its core game mechanics are pretty simple—players bid on the number of a given symbol or color they think is in each player's hands. Each player must, in turn, raise the bid or challenge the previous bidder. If you lose a challenge, you lose a card for the next hand. The last player with cards left wins.

The game took about eighteen months to develop, but the mechanics were complete within the first six months. What took so long was figuring out the theme and look for the game.

The game is easy to learn and quick to play, making it appropriate for families. It also has strategic bluffing and hand-reading elements that appeal to core gamers. We wanted a theme that could help us reach both audiences. We went through many iterations before settling on the final design.

Here are some behind-the-scenes looks at the themes we developed along the way.

The above designs clockwise from top left were called: *Liar's Cards*, *Are We There Yeti?*, *Schrödinger's Hats*, and *8-bit Crook*.

High resolution images of the above cards can be found at thinklikeagamedesigner.com/media. As you can see, each has a very different look and feel, potentially appealing to different audiences. We even took the *Schrödinger's Hats* prototype to a convention to get direct feedback from customers before finally deciding on *You Gotta Be Kitten Me*. It turns out a lot of people don't know who Schrödinger is, and trying to explain quantum mechanics during your game demo is a bad idea.

Designing a theme is just like designing a game. You should go through the entire core design loop when ideating and testing your new themes, getting feedback along the way until you find the right one.

ART, NAMES, STORY

Once you've decided on a theme, the next step is to commission art and flesh out each component into a full character in whatever world you've created. This is where the 6-cost creature with 6-attack and 4-health becomes a "Craw Wurm" and where abstract numbers and effects become dragons, spaceships, and kittens.

Much like when building structure during your initial design process, when building a story for your game, try to build structure into your characters, art, and background. This structure helps your world come alive and gives players things to discover as they dig deeper into your universe. Some tips include:

- Have a bigger story in mind. Put your characters into context and set expectations that can pay off later.

- Have key characters and locations recur to reinforce their importance (e.g., in art pieces, names, etc.).

- Create cycles with names and art that parallel mechanics (e.g., The Apprentice cycle in *Ascension* includes all 1-cost heroes that show a novice training in their respective faction).

- Seed evocative references in your names and story text. The players may not know what they mean, but they will be intrigued to learn more (e.g., Oros, Deepwood's Chosen; Freyalise, Llanowar's Fury, etc.).

How deep you want to go in telling a story very much depends on the type of game you want to build. *You Gotta Be Kitten Me* doesn't need much beyond an abstract theme and some cute animal images. A Triple-A video game (one with the highest level production and promotion budget) will require months of storyboarding and planning before any final art and graphics are commissioned.

When building games I plan to expand on, I try to have at least three years of story sketched out before the first release. This helps as I design future releases, and it keeps my fictional world coherent. Even if you never deliver on the complete story, the structure is valuable to guide your decisions. As Tyler Tichelaar, author of The Children of Arthur historical fantasy series, told me, "It's always best to have the rough draft of all the books in a series written before you publish the first one so you can ensure there are no inconsistencies." It's great advice that can be applied to game design as well.

USER INTERFACE, GRAPHIC DESIGN, AND LAYOUT

A User Interface (UI) is a fancy way of saying "How the user interacts with the game." Most people think of video games when they think of UI, but board games have a UI too! The size of a board, the pips on the side of a die, and the layout of a card all should receive the same level of thought you would put into a menu bar or character information screen in an RPG. A good UI can take complicated information and make it easy for a player to understand. A bad UI can take even the simplest game and make it impossible to play.

All good UIs have the following goals:

- Make it obvious what options a user has
- Make it easy to find the option a user wants
- Make a user want to interact with it

Building a simple and intuitive user interface is a complex and time-consuming design task. It will require its own design loops to test and iterate to find out what works best for your game. Take the time to iterate and learn what works and what doesn't.

Over time, your instinct for good and bad UI will get better. To help develop this intuition, *pay attention to interactions you have throughout your life, not just in games!* Notice that my description of good UI above doesn't just say "player." Anyone who uses any designed object has experienced good and bad UI!

Think about a teapot's interface. It has an obvious place to hold it so you don't get burned and a mechanism for making clear when it is time to pour tea. The best teapots are beautiful and draw you into them, while others are purely utilitarian and convenient for travel. Learn to notice the objects around you and see how some interactions are obvious and direct, while others require learning and training before they become clear. Some interfaces draw you in and others subtly repel you. Constantly ask yourself why things are designed the way they are to help train your instincts for making your own beautiful and intuitive interfaces.

TIPS FOR BUILDING GREAT UI

Here are a few tips to help focus your UI design process:

1. Priority rank each piece of information in order (e.g., attack, health rating, weapon durability, name). Make sure your design emphasizes the right information. Do the same thing with interaction points (attack buttons, power-ups, menu options, etc.)

2. Avoid clutter as much as possible. Avoid adding extra flourishes, symbols, and components that don't serve a purpose for the player. Less is more.

3. Draw the eye to the most important information and interaction points. Good layout should naturally make the player want to do what he or she is supposed to do.

A final great trick for testing your UI's effectiveness is to give players the game without any instruction. See how they interact and what they assume are the correct things to do. That doesn't mean your game needs to be playable without instructions, but you can learn a lot from watching players struggle to figure things out on their own. *If player instincts about what to do are generally correct and players seem happy to spend a fair amount of time interacting with the system to try to figure it out, you are on the right track!*

TEMPLATING AND COMPREHENSIVE RULES

For me, building out story, characters, and art is a fun process. It reminds me of my old days of playing *Dungeons and Dragons*. Creating worlds, characters, and epic plots are some of the things I love most about my job.

The last piece of polish, however, is a bit more of a grind. When first working on a game, I will use a lot of shorthand for what a game piece does. Everyone in my playgroup knows what I mean, and if they don't, I can always clarify.

In the real world, players won't have your same background assumptions, and you won't be in the room to answer their questions. Therefore, it is important to have a clear, consistent template for your text to help avoid confusion.

TEMPLATING

Templating is just a fancy word for "words and the order you put them in." While UI is how you communicate information graphically, templating is how you communicate information textually. Anyone who has gotten into an argument with a loved one knows that communication is hard in the best of circumstances, and trying to communicate your ideas to people whom you will never meet using only a few words on pieces of cardboard or a screen is even harder.

A Note on Collectible Games

The beauty of a collectible game is that each card and component is able to change the rules and thus create an ever-changing play experience. But when each card can change the rules, it is more important than ever to be clear and precise when describing each card's effect. Being precise with your templating helps players access your game and understand what is going on.

For physical games, language precision is about answering four basic questions:

Target: Who does the effect apply to?

Timing: When does the effect happen?

Script: What does the effect do?

Source: Who/what is the originator of the effect and what traits does it have?

Answering these questions thoroughly can lead to some long and cumbersome text boxes. In some games, the answers to the above questions will be implied (e.g., all card effects happen instantly when played) or irrelevant (e.g., the source of an ability is never referenced in the game). Other times, however, you will need to be clear with all of the information so players can make informed decisions.

You will have to make trade-offs when deciding how to template your effects and rules. Clarity, cleanliness, and consistency must all be considered during this process, and you will often have to sacrifice one of them in service to the others. Let's review some of the thought processes you should be undergoing as you develop templating for your game.

Concision vs. Clarity

Answering the basic questions above in detail and with precision can be cumbersome. Consider the following example of two templates of the same effect:

Template 1: Deal 3, Draw 3

Template 2: First, this card removes three health from target creature or player of your choice. Then, you draw 3 cards from your deck.

The second text is five times as long, but clearer. Which template is better? That depends a lot on your audience and the nature of your game. How relevant is each piece of information? How likely are your players to infer information you don't want to spell out? Can you imagine game scenarios where this template would be confusing?

Wrestling with these questions has led to many heated debates around our office because, as silly as the distinction may seem, your early decisions in templating will have long-reaching effects on the types of abilities you can create later and how your audience relates to them. If you choose never to identify source, for example, it will be harder to create future mechanics that reference it.

Keywords and Text Compression

A common tactic in games that introduce a mechanic used multiple times is to compress the rules text into a keyword. Keywords are special game jargon that stand in place of a bunch of regular text. Sometimes, keywords are converted into an icon and don't use text at all! The best keywords compress a lot of text into a word or symbol that is evocative of the effect.

A great example is the keyword "Flying" in *Magic: The Gathering*. Here are the comprehensive rules for Flying:

- 702.9. Flying
- 702.9a Flying is an evasion ability.
- 702.9b A creature with flying can't be blocked except by creatures with flying and/or reach. A creature with flying can block a creature with or without flying. (See rule 509, "Declare Blockers Step," and rule 702.17, "Reach.")
- 702.9c Multiple instances of flying on the same creature are redundant.

That is a mouthful! Most players, however, will simply intuit what flying means—creatures with flying can fly over creatures without flying. That one word compresses a lot of text in a way that doesn't confuse the player. Try whenever possible to use keywords that evoke the feeling of the effects you are trying to describe.

Physical vs. Digital Games

Because digital games enforce the rules for you, the importance of consistency and clarity in templating is reduced, though not eliminated. In digital games, it is generally preferable to use less precise but more readable language. Players will learn the ins and outs of the game by playing.

SHIP IT!

One of the biggest challenges with any game design process is deciding when your game is "done." More time can always be spent refining, polishing, and improving your design. It is worth spending time to make your game as good as it can be, but be careful not to let "perfect" be the enemy of good. *A good, completed game is infinitely better than a theoretically perfect game that never gets published.*

The most powerful way to ensure your game gets completed is to set a deadline. When you have a boss or a design contract, the deadline is often set for you. If you are working on your own game, set a deadline for yourself. Work toward that date as though you were delivering it to a client or your boss; then you'll be amazed how quickly you can get things done. That's not to say you will never miss a deadline (I've missed many), but treating them seriously forces you to focus on what is important and keeps your game moving forward until it becomes something you will be proud to have in players' hands!

PART IV

Building Great Games

. . . .

CHAPTER 17

What Makes Games Great?

So far, we've spent a lot of time reviewing the process of making games. Following this process and asking the right questions along the way is the work of game design. But at this point, it's worth digging a bit deeper into what makes games great.

The principle from Chapter 1 remains paramount: The player experience is what matters most. Part IV will review the player experience through five paradigms, each answering a key question about the experience.

Elegance: How aesthetically pleasing is the experience?

Excitement: How emotionally charged is the experience?

Depth: How intellectually stimulating is the experience?

Motivation: What gets players invested in the experience?

Engagement: How well does the experience hold players' attention?

These elements are powerful frames through which we can judge our players' experiences. Very often, you will need to make trade-offs between these different values as you work on your design. The best "aha" moments as a designer are when you find new mechanics, themes, or ideas that improve one or more of these elements without sacrificing another. But most often, it is about the subtleties of making good trade-offs depending on your target audience and the experiences most core to your game.

Let's dig deeper into each element and see how we can use them to make great games.

CHAPTER 18

Elegance

"Simplicity is the ultimate sophistication."

— **Leonardo Da Vinci**

Elegance is an aspect of aesthetics most often felt on an unconscious level. When experiencing elegance, we find ourselves uplifted and happy, but we aren't always sure why. Elegance is the quality of being pleasingly ingenious and simple. Elegant games achieve a depth of strategy and emotion with a minimal number of rules and components.

We've all played games that lacked elegance. These games have many bits and pieces, lots of strange exceptions to the rules, a clunky User Interface, and too many icons that don't make any sense. Sometimes, these clunky pieces are worth including, but usually, they detract from the overall game. *Great designs include only what is absolutely necessary.* The work of a game designer is very similar to that of a sculptor. Chip away at all the excess until only elegant beauty remains.

Practically speaking, how do we achieve elegance in our games? I believe there are four principles that can help.

1. Have as Few Rules as Possible
2. Have as Few Components as Necessary
3. Chunk Information
4. Teach in Steps

Let's look at each one in detail.

1. HAVE AS FEW RULES AS POSSIBLE

We gain pleasure from seeing a depth of strategy emerge from simple rules. Once you've identified your core mechanic, only add rules that support and highlight that mechanic and cut out anything that gets in the way.

Perhaps the greatest example of elegant design is the classic strategy game *Go*. *Go* rules are stunningly simple:

1. Black goes first.
2. Take turns placing stones.
3. Surround the most territory.

One rule for how to start, one rule for how to play, and one rule for how to win. It's hard to imagine a more elegant ruleset. There are a few more rules to deal with special situations that arise, but the fundamentals are all encapsulated above. Yet, despite the simplicity of the rules, *Go* has far more permutations and complexities than even games like chess. It took computers an additional twenty-five years after beating the best human chess player to beat the best human *Go* player.

Digital games can also accomplish this goal. In the game *Katamari Damacy*, you roll a ball around trying to absorb things smaller than you while avoiding things bigger than you. As you absorb things, you get bigger and thus grow from the size of a mouse into a monstrous world destroyer! The sense of relative growth and advancement creates an engaging experience almost by itself.

Similarly, in the game *Portal*, the player's primary tool is the portal gun. The portal gun shoots first one location, then a second, and creates a portal between the two targets. This simple tool then gets highlighted through a variety of contexts, which creates a huge depth of play (e.g., moving objects, using gravity to accelerate and change directions, trapping enemies, etc.). These different contexts present puzzles for the players to solve and many hours of enjoyment. *Portal* is a great illustration of a trick to elegant design: context shifting. Context shifting is when you take one thing and force people to look at it from a different perspective, creating new experiences without new rules. When you analyze your core mechanic, try to think about contexts that can highlight it in different ways.

2. HAVE AS FEW COMPONENTS AS NECESSARY

Perhaps you can relate to this experience. You open up a new board game and find dozens of pieces that clutter your tabletop. As a game designer, I've played countless games where I've had this experience and immediately regretted trying out the new game. Perhaps you've started playing a new console game where the number of buttons to press for commands felt overwhelming. Or a PC game with so many menu options on the screen (I'm looking at you *Total Annihilation*) that you are pretty sure you could fly a jet engine with less options.

Each additional piece, button, or menu choice is a sacrifice of elegance, and more importantly, another opportunity for players to disconnect from your game. For each additional component, ask yourself whether it absolutely needs to exist to support gameplay. Is there a way to do more with less?

Reducing rules will often lead to fewer components, but the same strategy of context shifting can also help ensure you use each part of your game to its greatest effectiveness. Ask yourself: What are the different ways I can use the same tools to accomplish my goals? One great example of context shifting is found in the *Star Wars Customizable Card Game*. It uses cards for a variety of purposes beyond just shuffling and drawing. Cards in the deck are set aside as a resource to play cards from your hand, running out of cards causes you to lose the game, and the top card of the deck is often revealed to randomize combat. Similarly, the card game for *Eve Online* uses card orientation to track the "build time" for a ship, as well as to track standing orders given to a ship. Each of the above mechanics could be done with tokens or pen and paper, but by viewing the cards in different contexts (e.g., orientation, location, counting total remaining, etc.), these games reduce their components and increase perceived elegance. *Compress more play into less things.*

3. CHUNK INFORMATION

Our brains have a funny way of looking at the world. Memorizing (or even reading) a string of numbers like 5558250987 can be very difficult. But take those same numbers and break them into chunks, 555-825-0987, and suddenly, they become easier to process and retain. What happened there? Our brains can retain only a few things at a time, but when that information can be grouped or "chunked" into separate units, each unit becomes a single item to process, thus making it possible for your brain to process more units in total.

This process is even more effective when chunks correspond to things you already know. Learning a phone number with the same area code as yours, for example, is much easier than learning one from somewhere new.

A similar thing happens when you try to learn a new game. The more that information can be presented in chunks and the more it can relate to things your players already know, the better. Following are three ways to use chunking to your advantage as a designer.

1. Chunking via Theme

One of the most common and powerful ways to chunk information in games is through your game's theme. For example, if a character in your game is called a Wizard, that will automatically create associations in the player. Players are likely to expect that this character can cast spells, has little armor, has a mana resource, etc. You can use these preconceived notions to your advantage to make even the most complex mechanics seem like an elegant, unified whole.

2. Chunking via Organization

When teaching new concepts, presenting them in an organized format that is familiar to the player will make it easier to understand. If all new characters have the same stats (e.g., Strength, Intelligence, Speed, etc.), it becomes easier to evaluate any new characters that show up in a game. When playing a first-person shooter, players expect that new weapons will function differently, but by knowing that they will all typically have some type of range, damage, and ammunition displayed in the lower left-hand corner of the screen, it becomes easier to understand how a new weapon might work. The organizational similarity helps each new piece of information become evaluated in the context of the information players already have.

3. Chunking via Image

Images are easier to process than words. Whenever possible, find images that bring to mind what you are trying to teach. Iconography is a powerful tool to get people understanding concepts without needing explanation.

If I see a disk icon in the corner of my screen, I can feel pretty confident that is how I save the game.

Similarly, if I see a sword icon next to a game stat, I can guess that the stat probably has something to do with combat. By thinking about the associations a player already has, you can make complex systems more elegant.

4. Teach in Steps

The human brain is capable of incredible things, but if you throw too much at it at once, it will become overwhelmed and shut down. The best games have a smooth ramp up where new skills and information are slowly acquired and mastered.

World of Warcraft is a very complicated game, with dozens of choices to make at any moment as a top level character. If you began the game with all the options of a top level player, it would be overwhelming. But because each skill is gained one or two at a time, a new player is able to process a relatively complex set of information. *Great tutorials are crucial for complex games.* Often, removing pieces of your game until later stages can help with the learning process and increase perceived elegance.

Elegance comes down to a simple principle. *Do more with less.* Think of your games as well-crafted poems. Calibrate each word choice, every rule, and every component for maximum impact, and mercilessly remove anything unnecessary to let your core vision shine.

CHAPTER 19

Excitement

"Time's up, let's do this!"

— Leeroy Jenkins

A bead of sweat forms on your brow. Your breath quickens. You've been playing solid poker for hours. You have a good hand and have been raising while others just called. Suddenly, the chip leader sitting to your right raises all in. You think you have him beat, but are you willing to risk it all to see whether you are right?

I don't know about you, but my heart rate goes up just imagining this situation. I can feel the tension and am intensely focused on what will happen next. These feelings are some of the most important for making your games engaging and memorable.

This feeling is excitement.

This is how you want your players to feel.

Two powerful tools can be added to your game to increase excitement—if you use them correctly. Those tools are Randomness and Big Moments.

RANDOMNESS

The simplest way to add excitement and uncertainty is to introduce randomness into a game. Randomness is any uncertain occurrence in a game that is not fully under player control. A shuffled deck, rolled die, and a critical hit chance are all tried and true tools to create exciting moments. Randomness can also greatly increase the novelty of play available in your game as the number of unique situations a player encounters increases.

Here are three considerations for adding randomness to your game:

1. Perception of Skill

When introducing randomness, it is important to be conscious of the trade-off against perception of skill. Games can be anywhere on the spectrum from pure skill (e.g., chess, *Go*) to pure randomness (e.g., *Chutes and Ladders*, *Left Center Right*). In most games, it will be important to keep at least the perception of player skill relatively high, even if there is a lot of randomness in outcome.

In order to keep perception of player skill high, give players meaningful choices that give them a feeling of control over the randomness. Classically, you should allow players to opt for a choice between a safer play with lower upside, or a riskier play with higher rewards. Players opting into a risk (e.g., choosing to stay in a poker hand on the hope of drawing a needed card rather than fold), will feel more in control of the outcome.

2. Reinforcement Schedule

When giving out rewards (e.g., loot drops on a monster), a classic psychological tool is to use a random reinforcement mechanism that rewards often early in the game, but with more spaced out higher level rewards as the game progresses. This type of variance reinforces the game's addictiveness. Such tools, when used responsibly, can make your games more compelling over the long term. Never knowing exactly when a desired reward will arrive makes the reward more exciting than a predictable outcome. I won't go deep into the moral discussion of addictive systems here, but suffice to say, if the only compelling thing about your game is an addictive reward system, you probably aren't on the right track.

3. Size of the Swings

Make sure that the impact of randomness is proportionate to its probability. If every turn, the players' positions are completely reset due to randomness, players will feel little to no agency in the game and lose interest. Past progress (whether earned via skill or randomness) must be respected as a game draws to its conclusion. The possibility of huge swings (e.g., a player in last place moving to first place on the last turn of a game) is a great feature, but only if it occurs rarely.

This ties into the next major tool to generate excitement: Big Moments.

BIG MOMENTS

Every game tells a story. In the best games, as in the best stories, there is a feeling of rising tension until a climax, in which a series of events culminates in an uncertain and exciting outcome. Creating a system to engineer these Big Moments is a fundamental skill of good game design. Following are two examples, "The Bomb" and "Agonizing Decisions," of how to create Big Moments.

1. The Bomb

"The Bomb" is a phrase describing a game mechanic or event that disproportionately affects the game's outcome. The key features of a bomb are:

1.   A single decision will have a hugely disproportionate impact on the game's outcome.
2.   Players are not certain exactly which decision will have this impact.

Classic bomb mechanics are "winner takes all" majority control systems, character deaths in video games, randomly appearing enemies, and time-limited power-ups. Hidden information of some kind (e.g., opponent cards in hand, uncertain end game timing, an unknown enemy around the next corner, etc.) is critical to setting up a proper "Bomb" and keeping tension in the game high.

2. Agonizing Choice

One of the most important and unique traits of games is their interaction with player choice. Some of the most exciting moments in games come when a player must make a difficult decision that will have significant ramifications on how the game will play out.

The choice is agonizing because its outcome is uncertain. The player feels the pain of making the decision, which sets up the joy of victory or the agony of defeat that will follow. Sometimes, these are split-second decisions such as when to run from an enemy or stay to fight when health is low. Sometimes, these are carefully thought-out moves as in a chess match.

In order for a choice to be agonizing, the outcome must be unclear. Unclear outcomes primarily stem from three sources:

1. Hidden information (e.g., cards in another player's hand, the outcome of a die role)
2. Player contingent decisions (If I throw rock, will he throw paper?)
3. Complex decision trees (If I move my bishop, what permutations will be possible?)

We play games in part to immerse ourselves in challenges that have emotional impacts without serious real-world consequences. *The agonizing choice is paradoxically painful and joyful, but it lies at the core of what makes games engaging.*

Excitement and uncertainty keep us engaged and help us reach that state of flow where we are pushed to the edge of our ability and live fully in the present moment. This is a joyous experience and one of the best gifts that games as an art form can provide. Play around with the above tools to see whether you can spice up your own designs.

CHAPTER 20

Depth

"Learning never exhausts the mind."
— **Leonardo da Vinci**

The human brain loves learning. We are programmed from years of evolution to find the most efficient way to solve a problem and latch on to it. One of the joys of playing games is exploring the decision space and finding ways to improve your strategy. Once an optimal strategy is found, however, the brain will stop being stimulated by a problem, so the experience quickly becomes boring and routine. The ideal target for game depth is a steady progression of learning throughout the play experience so that strategy and optimization are revealed constantly as a player explores, stimulating both the novice and expert brain alike.

When building depth into your game, keep your target audience in mind and recognize that adding depth to your game usually comes with the price of complexity and loss of elegance. Making good decisions about tradeoffs between depth and complexity is a skill that comes with practice, but in this chapter, we will explore the tools available to create depth in your games. Experiment with them to see what fits right in your own designs.

PLAYER PSYCHOLOGY

The greatest and most common source of depth is opposing player psychology. The human mind is a wonderfully complex object of study. Evolution has programmed us to be intensely interested in learning how other people think. Putting human psychology at your game's core is a great way to ensure depth. How do you do this?

1. Counterstrategies

Every strategy in your game should have a counterstrategy that can defeat it. Look at a game as simple as rock-paper-scissors. The game rules are trivially easy—each player simultaneously chooses rock, paper, or scissors. Scissors beats paper, paper beats rock, and rock beats scissors. Despite this simplicity, there are annual rock-paper-scissors championships and highly competitive players who play the game for years. The game's entirety rests in deducing the precise psychological state of your opponent and staying *exactly* one step ahead of him or her. Whenever I design a game, I always try to incorporate a rock-paper-scissors element into the high-end strategy to ensure long-term depth. For any strategy you enable in your game, make sure another strategy is dominant against it.

2. Hidden, Asymmetrical Information

By selectively giving information out to some players and not others, players will be driven to "read" the information known to their opponents based on their actions. Perhaps the greatest use of hidden information to develop game depth is found in poker. The mathematical probabilities of a game of poker are relatively straightforward, but the true skill comes in being able to discern which cards each player holds while concealing your own. This mechanic taps into our deep-seated need to learn and predict others' behavior. Deviating from the mathematically "best" strategy in order to deceive opponents about your game position greatly increases the variety of possible strategies, greatly increasing game depth. Give players access to exclusive information and give them opportunities to make a series of public decisions based on that information to utilize this tactic.

3. Personal Revelation/Discovery

Games can acquire depth by forcing people to make connections and reveal personal details about themselves and their lives. Unlike the two strategies above, personal revelation taps into a more social (rather than strategic) side of psychology. Party games like *Apples to Apples*, *What Were You Thinking*, and *Taboo* all take advantage of this mechanic. In *Apples to Apples* (as well as its more profane counterpart *Cards Against Humanity*), one player each round is listed as the "judge" and reveals an attribute card (e.g., Happy). Other players must play noun cards (e.g., Bill Clinton, Rollercoaster, etc.) that they think the judge will most associate with the attribute card. The judge picks the winner, and then play rotates to the next player as the judge. Forcing players to get into the head of fellow players triggers this same need to understand others, but in a more friendly and social context. Personal Revelation/Discovery mechanics can be added to a game by either:

A. Restricting communication channels (e.g., *Taboo*, *Pictionary*)

B. Setting goals that hinge on other player preferences (e.g., *What Were You Thinking?*, *Apples to Apples*)

TIME-RESTRICTED DECISIONS

Even relatively simple decisions become deep when they are made under a time constraint. Learning a basic attack move in *God of War* is easy, but applying it successfully to dozens of enemies simultaneously is a more engaging challenge. In the pattern matching game *Set*, each player must identify three cards that do not have any two traits in common. As soon as a player sees a pattern, she yells "Set!" and grabs the cards off the table, denying other players the chance to grab the set.

Time challenges against other players, automated obstacles, or a countdown timer can transform basic mechanics into deep learning experiences as players constantly try to improve on their reaction times and expertise with a skill. Even after mastering a skill, players can always try to "beat their best time" and thus continue to find challenge in a game mechanic.

When relying on time restrictions to increase game depth, it is important to keep the decision space simple. When complex decisions need to be made in a short amount of time, players may become overwhelmed and lose interest in the game.

COMPLEX DECISION SPACE

Complex decision space is the kind of depth people usually think of when they think about "deep" games. This kind of depth can have people staring for hours at a chessboard, planning five moves ahead, and considering all permutations. Complex decision space comes from having a lot of options and possibilities to consider before making a move. The more options, the harder it is to figure out the final game resolution.

Complex decision space is the type of complexity measured by computer processing power. Increasing the total number of permutations available to players will increase game depth. This can be done easily by increasing the number of rules and mechanics within a game. As we discussed in Chapter 18: Elegance, however, adding rules and mechanics reduces your game's perceived elegance. Thus, we want to look at other tools besides adding extra rules to create complex decision space. The best tools are probabilistic outcomes and exponential decision trees.

PROBABILISTIC OUTCOMES

Imagine playing a video game in which every time you land on a certain spot, a monster jumps out and attacks you. What do you do? Simple—don't go to that spot, or be ready before you do! If the monster only probabilistically attacks, however, it will take far longer for players to realize the correct strategy. Similarly, games involving dice, a shuffled deck of cards, etc. force players to consider a wide range of possible outcomes when determining the correct strategy.

EXPONENTIAL DECISION TREES

The game *Go* has some of the most elegant rules in the history of game design, yet it has more possible game states than chess. By allowing for a large variety of possible moves on any given turn, the planning for future moves becomes more and more difficult. Be aware that creating a large variety of possibilities can be a dangerous tool. If moves become too obscure, players will have difficulty connecting their early game decisions to an overarching strategy. This complexity can cause players to lose interest in the game and quit. Thus, with exponential decision trees, it becomes even more important to have interim goals and guidelines to give people a feeling of making progress and to help direct players.

Game depth is often presented as opposing game elegance and simplicity. Clever utilization of the above tools, however, can help ease this dichotomy. Remember that more depth is not always better. You need to custom-tailor your game's depth to the audience you are trying to reach. Making a deeper version of *Chutes and Ladders* misses the game's point. The best games are "easy to learn, difficult to master" for their target audience. Know your audience and experiment with your core mechanic to find that critical balance.

EXERCISE

Take a simple game you know (e.g., tic-tac-toe) and use at least one of the above mechanisms to add depth to it. Go through the core design loop and see how it feels. What got better about the game? What got worse? In your mind, was the tradeoff between depth and complexity worth it?

For a great example, compare the card games *San Juan* and *Race for the Galaxy*. Both use role selection and tableau building, but *Race for the Galaxy* adds a lot more complexity in exchange for more depth. *San Juan* also provides an interesting comparison as the simplified version of *Puerto Rico*, a popular strategy board game.

EXERCISE

Now take a more complex game you know (e.g., *Settlers of Catan*) and try removing complexity so the game would be more appropriate for a younger/wider audience. In the process, identify the game's mechanical and emotional core and think about how you can keep that essence with less complexity.

In addition to the above-mentioned example of *Puerto Rico* and *San Juan*, you can also take a look at the conversion of the board game *Monopoly* into the simple fifteen-minute card game *Monopoly Deal* to see how the game's emotional core can be simplified.

CHAPTER 21

Motivation

"Motivation is the art of getting people to do what you want
them to do because they want to do it."

— **Dwight D. Eisenhower**

Being a great game designer requires understanding the
players' feelings and how game-playing experiences affect
them. An important corollary to that skill is understanding
player motivations. Why do people play games in the first
place? Why will they choose to play your game over a different one? What will they do when playing your game and
why? The best game designers know what players will do and
why they will do it, better than they do.

Many paradigms exist for breaking down player motiva-
tions. Richard Bartle, a game designer who worked on *Multi-
User Dungeons* (MUDs), grouped players into four categories
(Achiever, Explorer, Socializer, and Killer). Mark Rosewater,
Head of Design for *Magic: The Gathering*, broke psycho-
graphic categories down into Timmy, Johnny, and Spike.[1]

---

1. https://magic.wizards.com/en/articles/archive/making-magic/
timmy-johnny-and-spike-revisited-2006-03-20-2

Game Designer Mark Le Blanc broke motivations down into eight categories of pleasure.[2] I'm mentioning these examples because a study of player motivation is really a study of human motivation.

Learning about humans is endlessly fascinating! As a game designer, you get the privilege of being a lifelong student on the subject. Here are the categories as I define them:

Motivation:	Subtype 1	Subtype 2
Aspiration:	Competition	Achievement
Expression:	Customization	Roleplaying
Connection:	Socializing	Helping
Immersion:	Experiences	Story
Growth:	Learning	Rewards

I promise you that this list isn't perfect. That being said, even an imperfect categorization of player motivation is useful! Use this chart as a lens to review your games and improve their appeal to your core audience. Not every game should try to appeal to every motivation, but it is important to know where your game's motivational strengths lie so you can emphasize them and (if appropriate) shore up weaknesses.

Here are the categories in more detail.

ASPIRATION

Motto: "Let's see what I can do."

Aspiration is the drive to prove yourself and overcome challenges. Games are a valuable part of culture because they

2. http://www.cs.northwestern.edu/~hunicke/pubs/MDA.pdf

allow us to test our limits safely and see how we measure up without real-world consequences. Competition involves measuring up against other players, while Achievement is measuring up against yourself or non-personal benchmarks.

Two primary methods exist to engage the Aspirational motivations of players. The most important is to give everyone the opportunity to "win" regardless of skill level. But if everyone wins, how can winning be an achievement? The key is to have staged victories that can appeal to players of all skill levels. Reaching a new level or moving up a ladder ranking are both achievements, even if they are far below the top performance tiers. This is why most games use points and levels as a satisfying way to measure progress. Each small increment is an achievement and can help satisfy the Aspirational drive. Build in many stages of achievement to fulfill this motivation.

The competitive drive is heightened when you are playing against those close to you. Close, in this sense, can mean both in terms of skill level or interpersonal relationships. A competition against a friend means more than a competition against a stranger, and a competition against someone of close skill level is a lot more compelling than playing against someone much better or worse than you. When designing games with online matchmaking or leaderboards, make an effort to pair people and rank performance against those with similar skill levels. This gives people a feeling that they can win and will push them right to the edge of their ability, which is the sweet spot for achieving a timeless flow state and staying motivated to play "just one more game" to get to that next plateau.

EXPRESSION

Motto: "It's not whether you win or lose; it's how you play the game."

Expression is the desire to be your authentic self and to be seen by others. Giving players options to customize their characters or play styles feeds into this need. Customization can be incorporated into your games both in the classic sense (e.g., allowing you to pick different functional and cosmetic traits for your character) and the strategic sense. By allowing a variety of strategies in your game, you give people more opportunity to develop their personal play styles. The more players can customize their experience and the strategies they use, the more they will be able to express themselves through play.

For players primarily motivated by expression, it may seem strange that I categorize "roleplaying" as a subtype of expression. *Roleplaying is about pretending to be something you are not, but it is also about expressing a part of yourself that normally can't be expressed.* Being able to inhabit a character is one of the safest ways we can express parts of ourselves. When I pretend to be a mighty mech warrior from the future or a mystical wizard from a mythical past, I am able to express parts of my personality that must be repressed in day-to-day life. Creating roles and characters in your game that appeal to classic Jungian personality archetypes (e.g., Hero, Rebel, Sage, Ruler) allows players to experience this often neglected form of expression.[3]

---

3. For more Jungian archetypes see http://www.soulcraft.co/essays/the_12_common_archetypes.html

CONNECTION

Motto: "We are all in this together."

I became a gamer at my family dinner table. On countless nights, my dad would sit down with my siblings and me to play *Uno*, *Monopoly*, *Sorry*, or whatever other game caught our fancy that week. *It wasn't about the game itself; it was about the connection between us.* Even years into playing *Magic: The Gathering* professionally, it wasn't primarily the game or the prize money that kept me around; it was the bonds of friendship that developed between shuffles. We all desire to connect with others, and gaming culture has developed largely around people who often have trouble connecting in other ways. Games provide community, fellowship, and bonding in powerful ways that impact millions of lives.

Games facilitate connection by allowing players to communicate and help each other. This help can include mechanics like granting bonuses to allies, cooperative victories, and group allegiances (e.g., guilds). Build in lots of "win-win" opportunities, where multiple players can pair up or make a trade that helps to facilitate the feelings of camaraderie and connection.

IMMERSION

Motto: "Let's leave the world behind."

I've spoken very little about so called Triple-A games so far in this book. These games work under the same principles as other games, but they have much higher production value, including amazing graphics, sound, and dedicated story cut scenes. These games have the immersive power of a Hollywood movie. Being lost in an imaginary world is a powerful motivation, and it isn't just available to those with multi-million dollar budgets.

The heart of an immersive experience is telling a story. In games, players don't just follow along with a story. They get to become its author. Linear cut scenes in games like *Warcraft* and *God of War* are awesome, but the way my character grows and the choices I make during play are where the joy of immersion really shines. Forcing players to make difficult choices with real consequences is a powerful way to immerse them in the story of play. When you can craft Big Moments (see Excitement, above), you let players live out the drama of a Hero's Journey, facing challenges and the uncertainty of whether those challenges can be overcome.

GROWTH

Motto: "I'm always getting better."

Growth is the motivational hook that gets me the most. I love the feeling of learning and improving, and gaming scratches that itch more than anything else I've experienced. I was a philosophy major in college and loved learning new concepts of logic and how to think more clearly. I got hooked into playing *Magic* professionally because there was so much to explore and learn. I could see how each time I played, I learned something to help me play better the next time. The key to engaging the growth motivation in your designs is to provide lots of small opportunities for progress so players at each skill level can still learn something interesting.

This motivation can also be tapped by granting new rewards and abilities at regular intervals. It is easy to measure my progress when I see an experience bar filling up or accumulating points at the top of the screen. Granting players new abilities to master has the added effect of both generating a feeling of getting more powerful (growing) and of generating a new set of skills to learn.

All of the above motivations are present to varying degrees in all of us, but there are dominant themes in different demographics and play groups. Identify whom you want to appeal to most and make sure to have great motivational hooks for those players.

EXERCISE

Review a game you have designed or one you love to play. Take the lens of each motivational hook above and rate how well it appeals to each of the various player motivations. Now for each motivation, come up with a modification or mechanic to enhance that motivational appeal. Bonus points for running a playtest with one of these ideas!

CHAPTER 22

Engagement

"A good teacher, like a good entertainer, first must hold his audience's attention. Then he can teach his lesson."

— John Henrik Clarke

Engagement is a measure of how well a game keeps your attention. In many ways, this trait is derivative of other traits of great games discussed above. If your game is exciting, deep, elegant, and motivating, your players will be very engaged, at least some of the time. Even with the games that excel at these traits, however, you risk losing engagement if your players don't feel they have any reason to continue to pay attention.

This typically happens for one of three reasons:
1. Too much downtime
2. The game is too difficult or too easy
3. The player no longer feels he or she can win

These issues are solved by:
1. Reducing downtime

2. Adjusting difficulty

3. Reducing certainty of outcome

Let's take a look at each approach to increase engagement.

REDUCING DOWNTIME

Reducing downtime can be achieved in two ways.

1. Reduce the Action Gap

In multiplayer games, waiting for your turn to come around can lead you to feeling disengaged. Look for ways to reduce turn length or find ways to get players to engage even during opposing turns. Real-time games rarely face this challenge because players can always be reacting to what is happening. Turn-based games can improve by emulating the best features of real-time games. Look for ways players can react during opponents' turns or reduce the time between turns. Give players something shared to care about (e.g., a "hot" shared resource) to keep their attention on what happens.

Poker is a great example of a turn-based game that keeps attention acutely focused during opposing turns. Each turn is very short and requires only one decision (raise, call, fold). In addition, watching players for any clue as to their intentions and hidden cards is a big part of play, so players are always watching when others are preparing to act.

2. Reduce Grind

Grind is generally associated with online video games, but it can be found in all types of games. Anytime players are facing repetitive actions without a feeling of progress, they are stuck in grind. Some amount of grind can be good, giving players a chance to get used to new mechanics but too much will cause players to disengage. *Games are engaging when we feel we have meaningful choices and an opportunity to explore new outcomes.* If players are regularly tuning out or stopping play at certain points, look for ways to accelerate play or add new learning opportunities. Maybe killing five boars is enough to complete the quest instead of ten. Perhaps a power-up in the middle of the quest can change the play experience enough to maintain engagement. In board games, see whether you can cut out slow sections of play or accelerate turns when there isn't much new going on.

ADJUSTING DIFFICULTY

Adjusting difficulty can be achieved in three ways.

1. Explicit Adjustment

For many single player games, adjusting difficulty is as simple as selecting a more or less difficult mode. As a designer, you can give a player more or less resources and make challenges more or less difficult to let players opt in to the difficulty level they want. Some games even dynamically adjust difficulty based on how a player is doing. In some Mario games, for example, if a player dies too often in one area, she is given the option to skip over the section she is having trouble with. In the roleplaying game series *Elder Scrolls*, the challenge of some monsters is automatically adjusted based on player level and progress. Be careful with dynamic adjustment, however, because some players want more explicit control over the challenge's difficulty.

In multiplayer games, difficulty adjustment is often accomplished by giving one player an advantage. Golf gives each player a handicap that adjusts his or her final score accordingly. *Go* masters give their weaker opponents additional starting pieces before a game begins. These tools can all help ensure a balanced playing field and keep engagement during play.

2. Matchmaking

Matchmaking is the system of pairing players against each other for player vs. player competition. A good matchmaking system is helpful to ensure a proper level of challenge for all involved. Chess is famous for its Elo ranking system, which scores players based on past performance and allows you to pair against other players of similar rating. Most e-sports games have created modified variations on Elo to pair Player vs. Player matches properly. How you choose to build your matchmaking system, especially if prizes are awarded for high ranking or for performing well in tournaments, can have a huge impact on the feeling of competitive play.

During my time as a professional *Magic* player, the Elo rating was used to determine who would be invited to prestigious tournaments with a lot of money on the line. Because you lose Elo points whenever you lose a match, it was often good strategy to avoid playing any ranked games so you didn't risk your ranking prior to a big tournament. As a game designer, it is worth thinking through all the implications of the matchmaking system you use. Avoid creating systems that discourage your players from playing the game.

3. Personal Objectives and "Little Wins"

You don't always have to give everyone a chance to win to make people feel like winners. Small victories and personal mini-goals reduce the need for each player to feel like he or she can win the entire game. In a match of *Counter-Strike*, even if my team is doomed to lose, I can still try to get a personal high score or number of kills. My mentality shifts to my personal objective, which removes the sting of losing the game at large and keeps me engaged. Give players other stats or goals to track to help them build their own games within the game.

You can also build your mechanics so that each player makes progress toward personal strategic goals. Deckbuilding games are great at giving people "little wins" because each player's deck will get better continuously throughout the game, independent of how other players are doing. If a player is able to execute his strategy successfully and have a few good turns, the game can feel like a win, even without achieving ultimate victory. Think about what mini-strategic objectives your players can accomplish within your game's broader arch.

REDUCING CERTAINTY OF OUTCOME

Here are four ways you can reduce the certainty of outcome.

1. Comeback Mechanics

To encourage engagement, the opportunity should always exist for players remaining in the game to win. Few things are more frustrating than knowing with certainty that you have no chance to win a game, but you are being forced to continue playing. The longer your typical game length, the more important it is to have mechanics that make the outcome uncertain for longer. These are often known as comeback mechanics because they allow players to "come back" from a losing position to win the game.

One key tradeoff when evaluating comeback mechanics is the importance of early game decisions versus late game decisions. By magnifying the significance of late game decisions (e.g., offering more points in later rounds of a game), you can help players feel like they can still overcome an early game deficit.

It is important to balance the strength of comeback mechanics against the feeling that early game decisions are still impactful. It can be helpful to think of each phase of your game as its own mini-game (e.g., beginning, middle, end). The prize of each mini-game is an advantage to the winner in the game's next phase. Focus on each phase independently and make sure it is engaging and impactful on its own.

2. Random End Game

Randomness is another valuable tool to give players a feeling of engagement late in the game. Introducing even very small probabilities for outrageous outcomes (e.g., the player in last place taking the lead late in the game due to a "hot" run of dice rolls) can greatly increase excitement.

One form of randomness particularly effective in keeping engagement high is to make the timing of the endgame uncertain. In Reiner Knizia's board game *Ra*, the game ends whenever a certain number of Ra tiles are pulled. As more Ra tiles get pulled, the tension rises, but a lucky run of tiles can extend the game out, giving trailing players a chance to catch up to the leader. If you never know exactly when the game will end, you never know whether you still have time to catch up.

3. Hidden Information

Hiding information about the final score can also be a useful tool for keeping engagement high. Games like *Settlers of Catan* introduce hidden victory point cards to help obfuscate the final score. In my deckbuilding game *Ascension*, cards included in each player's deck are worth points at the end of the game. Since players acquire so many cards throughout the game, it is almost impossible to keep track of all the points in each player's deck. I could just as easily have made it so players get point tokens whenever they acquire cards, leaving all points in plain view, but this would have reduced excitement because the outcome would have been much more easily predicted before the game end.

4. Negative Feedback Loops

You can create explicit mechanics in your game to combat against the leader's advantage. The racing game *Mariokart* uses these tools very effectively. Players in last place are more likely to pick up valuable power-ups, including the Blue Shell, which always attacks the player in first place. However, mechanics that disadvantage the leader can be a turn-off for competitive players if they are not integrated well. Many videogames will increase your stats behind the scenes when you are low on health, increasing the likelihood that you will have a come-from-behind victory when it looks like you are near death.

In board games, a common negative feedback loop is player self-regulation. When one player is clearly winning at *Settlers of Catan*, other players can choose not to trade with her, making it harder for her to score more points. Similarly, in a multiplayer game like Richard Garfield's *King of Tokyo*, players can gang up on a leader to help keep that player's advantage in check. Player self-regulation has its own challenges, however, since politicking (aka whining) becomes a significant part of game play ("I'm not winning, she is," "Why does everyone always pick on me?" etc.). To incorporate self-regulation, simply give players the opportunity to benefit disproportionately (e.g., trade with) or harm (e.g., attack) players of their choosing. Other negative feedback loops in board games include making the leader pay more for resources (e.g., paying increased upkeep for workers in *Through the Ages*) and giving players in last place "first pick" of future resources.

As with all things game design, the key is to focus on how players feel. Come-back mechanics aim to keep players engaged and interested until the very last move. This engagement feeds into the most important feeling—the desire to come back and play again!

PART V

Making Money

· ·

CHAPTER 23

Monetizing Games

"Making money is art and working is art and
good business is the best art."

— Andy Warhol

The principles outlined in previous chapters are all you
need to be a great game designer who makes great games. For
some of you, the goal ends there. But for most of you, there is
another, critical piece of the puzzle: You need your games to
make money. This chapter shows you how to do that.

BEING A PROFESSIONAL

"Being a starving artist is a choice, not a necessary
condition of doing creative work."

— Jeff Goins

Only one thing separates professional game designers
from amateurs. *Professional designers make games that make
money.* That's what it means to be a professional. You get the

work done that lets you pay the bills. Otherwise, game design is a hobby. There is nothing wrong with being a hobbyist game designer, but if game design is something you want to pursue as a career, you need to wrestle with how to turn your designs into dollars.

When I finished college, I took a year off and did nothing but play *Magic: The Gathering* for a living. I won over $60,000 that year and had an amazing time traveling around the world, making new friends, and doing something I loved. I even started working on designing some of my own games for fun in my spare time.

But in my head, this was only a "gap year" because I was destined to go to law school (just like my parents) so I could get a "real job." I stopped playing games and went to NYU School of Law, where I spent an entire year being miserable. Fortunately for me, fate intervened. The summer after my first year of law school, I was offered an internship at a game company in San Diego. Working on games for a summer opened my eyes to what my life could be like, so I promptly quit law school and moved to San Diego to pursue my passion.

Though it seems like the obvious decision now, it wasn't an easy one to make at the time. I felt a lot of psychological pressure to stay on the beaten path. I was afraid I couldn't really make a career out of my love for gaming, and that fear almost stopped me from following my passion. I share this story in the hope that it inspires you to be bold and pursue your dreams, even if they seem impossible now.

MONEY MYTHS

Take a moment right now and assess how you feel about making money from game design. What images come to mind when you think about making games for money? Do you get excited? Do you think about working at a big company or doing things on your own? Do words like "sellout," "pay to win," and "corrupt" come to mind? Whether you understand it rationally or not, many of us have hangups when it comes to turning something we love into something we make money doing.

That you can't do great creative work when you are also trying to make a living is one of the most pernicious myths in our society. I love designing games, but if I couldn't make money doing it, I could perhaps design a handful of games in my lifetime that would likely only be played by my friends and family. Instead, I am able to work on dozens of games and bring joy to millions.

Making money from your art gets a bad rap in our society, so I want to help you squash any unconscious barriers that may be preventing you from following a career in design. You may have money scripts in your head that prevent you from allowing yourself even to think about making money from something you love!

Here are a few of those scripts that are pretty common:

- Money is the root of all evil.
- Real artists do it for the love, not the money.
- It's not the game designer's job to worry about making money.
- The business people will handle the money stuff.
- I'm not willing to "sell out."

I'm here to punch all those limiting beliefs in the face. Making money lets you make more games and get those games in front of more people. Your job as a game designer is to provide value and entertainment to your players. You can't do that if you don't have the finances to do so. If you do your job right, players will be happy to pay and support your work.

DESIGNING FOR DOLLARS

The best games integrate mechanics with monetization strategies in a seamless and enjoyable way. Your game's design will dictate whether it should be sold as a single purchase, a subscription model, a collectible game, or something else entirely. A great game designer needs to understand the interplay of his or her design with the marketplace.

Now, just because making money from games isn't evil doesn't mean that anything goes. There are ethical and unethical ways to make money. If your game is primarily designed to extract as much money from people as possible, you are not thinking about design (or business) correctly. *Your primary goal in design should be to deliver as much value as possible to your players.* That includes thinking about how they will pay for your games in a way that supports your work and feels fulfilling to them.

I have one cardinal rule I use when deciding whether I am on the right track when it comes to monetization. When making decisions, always ask yourself: "If I were the target audience, would I be thrilled to play and pay for this game?" If the joy and value you provide *far* outweighs the cost, then your customers will be happy to pay and eager for more. If you have any question that the value provided isn't worth the cost, keep working until you are sure beyond a doubt that you are making people's lives better. If you follow that rule, you are unlikely to go wrong.

Now that we've got the psychology of making money covered, let's get into the specifics.

CHAPTER 24

How to Be a Professional Game Designer

"The professional has learned that success, like happiness, comes as a by-product of work. The professional concentrates on the work and allows rewards to come or not come, whatever they like."

— Steven Pressfield

The question I get asked most often by fans and players at conventions is: How do I get a job in the gaming industry? If you are reading this book, the odds are good that you have a similar goal. The answer I always give is counterintuitive: *The easiest way to get paid in the game industry is not to get paid in the game industry.*

Despite sounding like a Zen riddle, the above answer is a great guideline for anyone new to the industry. What it means is that you should start doing work in games so you can prove yourself as someone worth hiring in the future. The gaming industry is competitive, and game companies are always on the lookout for pleasant, smart, hardworking people to help them be successful. Be one of those people and you will have no trouble finding a job in the long run.

LEARN FOR FREE

If you want skills that can help you in the industry, start practicing them and offering up the results. There are countless ways to do this. A few include:

- Practice writing skills by blogging game reviews and strategy articles and sending them to your favorite sites and game companies.

- Learn Photoshop by watching YouTube tutorials and creating useful game accessories, memes, and components. Then post your work online.

- Learn how to manage a community by becoming active on game forums and helping coordinate people there.

BUILD A RESUME FOR FREE

Think hard about your skills and find a niche that helps distinguish you from the crowd. By volunteering at your favorite companies, you will start to build a resume that can help you get a paying job. Keep an open mind about what areas of the industry can get your foot in the door. Lots of people want to be game designers, but game designers who can also program, do graphic design, manage projects, or write well are more likely to get jobs. Taking a job in a non-design position gives you the opportunity to begin working with game designers. This can quickly transition you into a game-design role if you show commitment and talent.

BUILD RELATIONSHIPS FOR FREE

"It's not what you know; it's who you know."

— Unknown

Success in any industry is not just about doing great work; it's also about building great relationships. Don't approach people with a cynical "I need to network" attitude, but with a genuine desire to connect. Tabletop games in particular (but online games as well) are growing in popularity because people have a desire to connect with others. Go to game conventions and offer to volunteer for your favorite companies. Find local Meetups for designers and get involved. Sitting around a gaming table at conventions and Meetups is a great way to build real relationships with people in the industry.

Be hard-working, kind, and personable. By being the kind of person others want to work with, you will be at the top of their minds when new opportunities arise. Give useful feedback on games other people make. Bring your own designs and show them to prospective players and publishers to get feedback. Thank them for their time and follow up afterward.

Relationship building is a long game. Find people you can genuinely connect with and build relationships with for life. Learning, gaining experience, and building relationships are fundamental to growth in any industry. Getting to do it while playing and being immersed in games is not only good for your career, but it's a great way to have fun and meet amazing people along the way!

CHAPTER 25

How Can I Get My Game Published?

"I had a period where I thought I might not be good enough to publish."

— **Stephen King**

To publish a tabletop game, you have two options:

1. **Sell Your Game to a Publisher:** This option allows you to spend more of your time on game design and less on running a business, but relies on other people to believe in and execute your vision.

2. **Self-Publish:** This option gives you more control over the final product and more profit if your game succeeds, but it costs a lot more time and money upfront. It is also harder to have a big success without a publisher behind you.

The choice of which path to pursue is a personal one, but I recommend you try selling your tabletop game first so you can learn what works and build a reputation before taking the more expensive and riskier path of self-publishing. This chapter will walk you through how to get your game sold to a publisher.

First, one word of caution: *Don't try to publish until you've got a great game!* Go through the core design loop multiple times. *Get a great reaction from playtesters you don't know.* Only then should you consider publishing.

Don't waste your time or a publisher's time until you've got a great game to pitch.

Now that I've got that out of the way, here are seven tips to help sell your game to a publisher.

1. Go to Conventions
2. Be Respectful
3. Have a Good Elevator Pitch
4. Explain Your Game in Fifteen Minutes or Less
5. Develop Relationships and Add Value
6. Take Feedback Well
7. Don't Focus on Money at First

Let's briefly look at each one.

1. GO TO CONVENTIONS

Pitching publishers at conventions is a very effective tactic. Game companies go to conventions to interact with players and meet with others in the industry. Often, people there can review your games or at least connect you to others who can. It is far harder to say no to someone in person than over email, and it is far easier to make a compelling pitch face-to-face. Research where the companies you love will be and go there! As of this writing, in the hobby gaming tabletop industry, the best shows for making your pitch are Gen Con in the United States and Spiel Essen in Europe.

2. BE RESPECTFUL

Publishers have many demands on their time and get a lot of game pitches. Be respectful and kind even if they don't have a chance to review your game. Ask for contact info and be ready to follow up after the show. Offer to send a copy of the game and rules for them to review. Make sure to write down and follow through on all the commitments you make! As a publisher, I won't usually spend much time on someone who brings me even a decent pitch. But if I see the person following up and making steady improvements over time, I'm almost certain to give him or her a shot.

3. HAVE A GOOD ELEVATOR PITCH

This point was covered in Chapter 5 about Inspiring, but it is worth repeating. Your game idea should be easy to communicate by referencing something the publisher will know and something original (e.g., it's a deckbuilding game with magic combat and plays in thirty minutes). Make sure your rules are written down so the game can be learned even if you aren't present. Nice-looking art and prototypes can help too, but they aren't necessary.

4. EXPLAIN YOUR GAME IN FIFTEEN MINUTES OR LESS

Publishers are busy, so they will judge your game in 5–15 minutes. If you can't get the core game loop across in fifteen minutes, you will not sell your game. That doesn't mean the game has to be playable in fifteen minutes, just that it can be explained and understood in that time. Practice explaining the game to friends before bringing it to a publisher.

5. DEVELOP RELATIONSHIPS AND ADD VALUE

Often, the best way to get in front of publishers is to volunteer. Contribute value by helping out at conventions, doing QA (Quality Assurance) testing, contributing articles and forum posts, etc. Don't expect payment or immediate return. *Be kind, communicate clearly, exceed expectations, and be overall great to work with.* Publishers will be *far* more likely to listen to your game pitch and help you get it to a purchasable point if they like you and you already provide value. *Building relationships and community is the most important thing you can do to ensure your long-term success.*

6. TAKE FEEDBACK WELL

If a publisher gives you feedback, don't argue with him or her! I see this all the time, and I can't believe how often it happens. Take the feedback, say "Thank you," and ask whether the person would be willing to review the game again if you addressed some of the issues. Everyone loves to have his or her opinion respected, and publishers will be more likely to take your game if they feel a sense of ownership and contribution to the final result.

7. DON'T FOCUS ON MONEY AT FIRST

Even in the best-case scenario, hobby game designers usually make only $1,000–$5,000 in initial purchase with 3–5 percent royalty on a game. Only a select few well-known designers do better than that. If you've never published a game before, expect to get the low end of that scale. When just starting out, it is more important to get your game published than to haggle with a publisher.

After you've established yourself with a successful game or two, it will become much easier to ask for more money on your future designs. The one thing you should negotiate for is to get the rights to your game back if it doesn't get published within a reasonable amount of time (e.g., two years) or if it goes out of print. This stipulation ensures your design doesn't get orphaned with a publisher who doesn't support it.

Your job as a designer is to get the publisher to try your game and be open to working with you. After that, it will come down to whether the publisher likes the game and whether it fits in its game portfolio. Do your homework to give yourself the best chances. Research the different publishers in your industry so you can pitch to those most likely to want the type of game you've designed.

Do not take it personally if a publisher doesn't want your game. Whether or not a publisher will take your game is ultimately out of your control. *Remember that building relationships with publishers is more important than what happens with any one game.* Keep working on improving your craft and building relationships and you will get a game published.

CHAPTER 26

Game Business Models

"I never called my work an 'art'. It's part of show business,
the business of building entertainment."

— Walt Disney

Back in the day, there was only one way to make money from games: invest a ton of money upfront and hope that stores would carry your game and customers would buy it. Today, we are lucky to live in a world where there are countless ways to monetize your games. Here is a short list:

- Single Purchase
- Expandable
- DLC (Downloadable Content)
- Free Demo with Unlockable Content
- Subscription
- Microtransaction
- Freemium
- Collectible
- Donation-Based
- Legacy/Destructible Games

And that is only the beginning! Each of these models can be mixed and matched within the same game for limitless possibilities. All these options put the burden on you as a designer to decide which model is best for your game. There is a lot to consider when making this decision, so we will only review a few here. Note as you read that many of these categories have overlaps, and your designs might rely on more than one model to generate revenue.

SINGLE PURCHASE

Single purchase is the classic model for selling games. You make a game, set a price, and once the game is purchased, it can be played in its entirety as many times as a player wants. Selling single purchase games requires your customers to make an investment upfront, often before they get a chance to play your game. This means that initial sales and marketing is more important than with any other model.

With single purchase games, your game hook needs to be compelling and obvious when viewed on a store shelf or in an online store. If you've got a big license (e.g., Marvel, Star Wars, Harry Potter), this shouldn't be a problem. If you don't have that kind of heavy-hitting intellectual property, you need to find a way to appeal to your target audience members before they get a chance to purchase and play your game. I recommend finding a core group of early adopters (it is often worth giving them free copies) who can become evangelists for your game, writing reviews, giving demos, and generally helping to persuade others to plop down hard-earned money on a game they haven't played yet. Eye-catching packaging and an easy-to-understand concept help a lot here as well.

EXPANDABLE

Expandable games include sequels, DLC content, and unlockable levels. Expansions allow you to increase a game's lifespan by providing new content to people who already love your game. It is usually wise to consider how your single purchase game might be expanded even before its release. Having some of those notes handy will come in useful if your game is a hit and you want to give fans more. I'll talk about the design thinking of expanding games in the chapter below on how to make games that last.

SUBSCRIPTION MODEL

Subscription-based games require players to pay at regular intervals to keep playing the game (typically monthly). Often a subscription comes with new content, but new content is not tied 1-1 with the subscription itself. (The more content is tied to each subscription payment, the closer your game becomes to other revenue models.) Subscription games make money by engaging a community over the long term. Unlike a single purchase or expandable game, where upfront impressions are most important, a subscription game must have a long tail of engagement to keep players happy and ensure solid monetization. Many subscription games use time-delay mechanics, also known as "grind" to engage players longer. As I mentioned earlier, grind forces players to complete repetitive actions or restricts how often an action can be performed to stretch out the game mechanics' lifespan. In most RPGs, character leveling stretches out over longer and longer periods with each higher level. Contrary to popular belief, some amount of grind can be a good thing. Whenever a player acquires new abilities or enters a new play zone, some repetitive interactions give him an opportunity to get used to the new play modes so he can fully appreciate them before moving on to the next new thing. Using grind purely as a tool to extend player lifespan, however, is not recommended. While these tactics are effective, they are not particularly compelling from a player perspective. Use them sparingly!

The two best strategies for keeping players engaged with a subscription-based design are social engagement and regular content. In order to keep players engaged in a game for the long term, you need to build a sense of community. I first started playing *Magic: The Gathering* because I found the game engaging and I enjoyed the competition. But I continued to play the game for over a decade not because of the gameplay, but because of the community. Meeting up with friends at the local card shop or at tournaments around the world built friendships that have lasted a lifetime. Similarly, many of us got hooked on *World of Warcraft*, not because the game was so innovative each month, but because all of our friends were playing and we could reliably connect with them in Azeroth. Building social mechanics into your game could be an entire book unto itself, but suffice to say this is a key goal for any subscription-based or collectible game you want to design. Look for opportunities to bring players together, allow them to help each other, and encourage collaboration and communication both during and between game sessions to build a strong community.

Developing regular content for your game in a subscription model is similar to the methods for developing content in other models. I cover most of that process in Chapter 27: How to Make Games That Last. The one additional factor to highlight in a subscription model is to consider seasonal content in addition to standard new content creation. Seasonal content gives players something to look forward to and changes the game up without necessarily requiring all new designs. An in-game "Holiday Festival" with events and challenges or a "Halloween Expansion Pack" can fulfill a role in giving players new ways to engage with your game to keep things fresh and interactive.

COLLECTIBLE GAMES

Collectible games are games where content is acquired in a random or semi-random way. Components of the game have scarcity (i.e., some components are rarer than others). Collectible games require the most "design thinking" of any business model because the collection process is itself a game. You need to ask the same kinds of questions about the player experience in collecting as you do about the play of the game itself. How does it feel when you open a booster pack looking for that ultra-rare card? What is the emotion around opening up a loot chest or hunting for a rare monster drop? An enormous number of variables need to be considered in this process. I'll highlight two here:

1. Outline Collection Requirements

When determining components for a collectible game, you need to decide how many components a player needs to play. Do you need three miniatures, sixty cards, or one champion? Think about what the experience will be like when the player has a small collection versus a large collection. Is it still fun to play when you don't have a lot of options? Is it still exciting to collect after you already have a few items? You can drive this excitement by ensuring your engine supports a variety of strategies and synergies between different subsets of the total available collection. Possessing the maximum number of copies of a single item also plays into feelings about collection. The more copies of a card you can use, the better it feels to collect those cards over the long term, but the more daunting it can seem to try to collect everything you need. The number of allowed copies also plays into collection variance within a game.

2. Target Collection Variation in Game

Having a novel experience in gameplay is important to long-term enjoyment. Collectible games are powerful ways to ensure novelty of play by constantly changing the game components available within a given game. In addition to determining how many components a player needs, you should also think about how many components show up in a given game.

As mentioned above, the number of copies of a single component allowed per player influences variation in game. The more copies, the less novelty of play. On the other hand, more copies allowed per game gives players a greater feeling of control over their collections and extends out the time that acquiring new copies is still exciting for a player.

If you always have all your components available each game (e.g., a miniatures game where all the figures start on the board), then games will tend to play out more similarly during repeat play. These games will likely want another randomization mechanic.

If you have too few components show up in a game (e.g., drawing only seven cards from a sixty-card deck), then players may not feel enough agency in their customization. This type of game will likely want little additional randomization or the introduction of other tools to select which collectible components are available (e.g., the ability to search your deck or redraw your starting set of cards).

There is no objectively right or wrong answer here. Play around with these numbers to find the balance between variance and predictability appropriate for your game and audience.

FREEMIUM

Freemium games are digital games with theoretically unlimited free content, supported by optional in-app purchases known as microtransactions. For business model analysis purposes, I separate these from expandable content like DLC levels. As of the writing of this book, microtransactions are the dominant form of payment for digital games, and they have warped the gaming industry significantly. Freemium games have a bad reputation and, in some cases, for good reason. Since the overwhelming majority of freemium game revenue comes from less than 1 percent of the players, game designers target these "whales" often to the detriment of other players. The worst of these designs exploit addictive tendencies and put up frustrating "pay walls," functionally preventing players from advancing without paying money. Games like *Candy Crush*, *Farmville*, and countless others have exploited these psychological tendencies to make money in ways I find unethical.

That being said, there are significant advantages to the microtransaction model for both players and designers. Since freemium games are free to download, players can sample a game without having to commit money. Players then have the option to commit as much time and/or money as they want to support the game. This sampling encourages a far larger community than would otherwise be possible since players who can't afford to pay money for a game can often afford to spend time instead. More players in your game builds a bigger community and makes it more likely your game will reach a sustainable "critical mass" of players.

When designing games for a freemium model, it's paramount that you balance the desire to make more money with the need for ethical design. Here are some rules of thumb I use to stay on the right track. These are not hard and fast rules, but they are useful guidelines for evaluating payments in your system.

1. Don't let people pay for an unfair advantage in the game. If you do, give free players a plausible path to acquire the same advantages.

2. Put a reasonable cap on the amount a player can spend. Limitless spending is a sign that you are preying on addictive tendencies.

3. Cosmetic upgrades are fair game as long as they still follow Rule #2.

These are my personal rules, and I'm sure some people will disagree with them. Games like *League of Legends* have had huge success generally following these rules. Although you won't earn as much money from each customer as you might using more exploitative designs, the loyalty you earn from your players will be far more valuable in the long run.

CHAPTER 27

How to Make Games That Last

"Art is never finished, only abandoned."

— Leonardo da Vinci

All of us dream of making games that will last for years. Of course, none of us can predict whether we will succeed. There are, however, steps we can take to prepare a game to stand the test of time. I've worked on multiple game properties that have continued to sell and produce content for seven or more years, and I've noticed trends among them that support a game's longevity.

My focus here is not just on making a game that is played for a long time, but on making a game where new content can be released regularly to keep players coming back for more. Although there are many ways to release new content, I'll group them all under the category "expandable games."

One paradoxical concept is critical to a successful long-term expandable game. That concept is "same but different." People play your original game because they love it. But if they are going to buy a new expansion, they want something similar to what they love, but different from what they already have. Good design requires a careful balance of these two contradictory desires.

I believe five basic principles are critical to a game's long-term success.

1. START WITH A SIMPLE, DEFINED CORE

Know what your game is about. What distinguishes your game from others in the market? What do players love most about your game? Any game that releases expansions will inevitably get more complicated over time. As you keep layering new mechanics and modifying old ones, holding on to your core is critical for keeping your game moving in the right direction. *If you stay true to your core, you can take your players places they never thought they would go, without losing the sense of what they loved about your game to begin with.*

The core of my deck-building game *Ascension* is adapting to the changing available cards and using those cards to modify your deck and execute your strategy. Each *Ascension* expansion provides a new angle to evaluate the available cards or new resources to balance against them. *Magic: The Gathering* is about the balance of the different colors and playing more powerful creatures and spells as you increase your mana from turn to turn. Each set plays with these core resources and forces players to pay attention to different elements.

2. FOR EACH EXPANSION, FIND THE HOOK THAT PLAYS WITH YOUR CORE

For each expansion, try to find the one- or two-sentence hook that will draw people to your game. What will make your players want the new expansion? Finding a good hook is not always easy, but good typical places to look are:

A. Designs cut from your initial release: In general, when you are working on a first release for an expandable game, you should cut out anything not essential and keep things as streamlined as possible. Those extra discarded features, however, are gold that can be mined for future expansions. In *Ascension: Storm of Souls*, we introduced Trophy Monsters, which allow you to control when you want to use a monster reward, rather than being forced to use them immediately. Trophy Monsters were part of the original *Ascension* game, but they were cut to reduce complexity.

B. Player Pain Points: Games are all about tension and key decision points. Tension is valuable because it creates drama in your game and a variety of outcomes, but the flipside of the joy of discovery and victory is the pain of frustration and loss. Players who enjoy your game are likely familiar with the pain points and difficult choices your game presents. Offering a solution to pain is a great way to get them excited about the new content. You can offer players freedom from that pain, but only if it comes with a new price and new form of tension to keep the game interesting.

Ascension: Dreamscape very directly addresses a common player pain point: the ever-changing center row. Regularly, players are forced to watch as their favorite card gets acquired or defeated by another player. Because Dreamscape cards are always available and only available to you, you can relax a bit and know that the card key to your strategy won't be lost. The new tension introduced is the Insight resource, which can be hoarded from turn to turn but is hard to acquire. Spending it at the right time and on the right card is key to victory.

3. FORCE PLAYERS TO REEVALUATE OLD CONCEPTS

Look at the elements in your game where the learning curve has flattened out. Almost all players who look to purchase expansion content have a lot of experience with your game. What "truths" that they take for granted can you disrupt? How can you force them to reevaluate their previously held assumptions? Common practice in collectible and expandable games is to take old staple effects and merge them with the new hook or mechanic.

In *Star Wars: Knights of the Old Republic*, the essence of the roleplaying game was making choices that bring you closer to the light side or the dark side and thus impact the story and choices available later. *Knights of the Old Republic II* expanded on this concept by giving players the ability to influence the light or dark side alignment of their companions, expanding on those stories and relationships and further reinforcing the importance of a player's own light or dark side choices.

Returning to my own designs, in *Ascension: Rise of Vigil*, we introduced treasure cards that stack up underneath a center row card and act as a bonus when that card is acquired or defeated. It is common practice in *Ascension* to buy the most expensive card you can, but now with treasure cards coming into play, it can sometimes be correct to buy a "worse" card in order to access the treasure underneath, forcing a reevaluation of the board depending on your need for that treasure. Similarly, in *Ascension: Dreamscape*, the Insight resource required for your Dream cards is only available when certain cards appear in the center row. How you evaluate those cards will depend on your personal selection of Dreams and current strategy.

4. ROTATE FOCUS

Each expansion to a game needs to add something new. Every new thing is something else that must be learned. Every new thing that has to be learned increases the barrier to entry for someone new to come into your game. While a good tutorial and slow introduction of new material can help, it will not solve the problem entirely. For a game to last many years, this problem must be addressed.

By rotating your focus and cycling mechanics in and out of your game, you can keep complexity at a manageable level and reuse old mechanical hooks in future expansions. A common mistake among designers is to try to include everything "cool" about a game in future expansions. Let certain mechanics rest for a while to keep complexity in check and to allow the new mechanics to shine. When you bring back old mechanics, older players get to enjoy the return of a favored mechanic, while new players do not have to deal with learning every mechanic from every release all at once.

5. LISTEN AND ENGAGE

No game can last for long without a community of players to support it. Listening to and engaging your players is the most important thing designers can do to help ensure their games stand the test of time. I played *Magic: The Gathering* professionally for several years, and although the game is great, it was the players and the community that made me a lifelong fan.

Don't think just about the mechanics of your game. Engage your community and encourage its members to engage with each other. This can be done through organized play tournaments, online streaming, giveaways, fan-created content, and more. Listen to what your players want and try to respond with things that will resonate with their needs (not necessarily their demands).

As you make expansions and try to resolve the "same but different" paradox, you will inevitably make some of your fans unhappy. "It's too similar to the last release" or "Mechanic XYZ ruins the game!" are phrases you will just have to get used to. Know that fans respond strongly because they care about your game. Learn to love even the hostile reactions. They are far better than deafening silence.

It is a great privilege to design games for a living, and showing gratitude to your players will help build that community and sense of trust so that even when you make an expansion they don't love, they will still have an interest in checking out the next one.

A FINAL NOTE

Living the Lessons

"Knowledge without action is futile."

— Abu Bakr

This is it, the end of the book! This is more than an ending, however. Use this knowledge to start your path to a career in game design, or to update your skills and launch a new project. Moreover, I hope the design process we've discussed helps you to create new things and solve problems in all areas of your life. There is always more to learn, but don't fall into the trap of thinking you need to learn more before you can begin. The only thing you need now is action!

You have all the tools you need to be a game designer right now. Practice the core design loop and keep an open, curious mind. You will make mistakes. You will make games you are embarrassed about later. But you will also learn. You will make new connections. You will be living the life of a game designer.

Are you ready?

EXERCISE

Commit RIGHT NOW to ten actions you will take within the next ninety days to bring at least one of your creative dreams to life. They can be as small as you want, but make a commitment now while the ideas are fresh in your mind, and start on the first one right away! It is through this step-by-step process that you will take what you've learned and turn it into reality. Write down your actions below:

_____

_____

_____

_____

_____

_____

_____

_____

_____

_____

In this book, you've learned how to overcome fear and get your creative projects started. You've learned the role of the game designer and how to apply the core design loop to your creative process. You've learned how to refine your designs and apply the principles of great games to your designs. You've learned how to break into the industry and find your niche.

If you apply the principles you've learned, you can create your own games, make a living doing it, and have fun along the way! Now that you've read this book, you have me in your corner to help you on your journey. You can text me directly at my personal number to schedule a complimentary

30-60 minute consultation: (760) 444-0797. Just start your text with the word "Commitment" so I know you've read the book. I want to support you in your designs and goals!

You can also reach out to me on Twitter @Justin_Gary or via email Justin@JustinGary.com. Let me know what you think of the book! Your feedback is invaluable and will help me refine this book for future printings. If you can, please leave a review at sites like Amazon to help others find this book as well. Genuine reviews from readers are the most powerful way to help spread the word and build on our community.

I want to see you succeed, so don't hesitate to reach out with questions or concerns or to schedule a free call to help with your design projects.

Thank you for taking this journey with me. I wish you much success, and I look forward to playing what you create and to learning more of the craft together with you.

ABOUT THE AUTHOR

Justin Gary is an award-winning game designer, entrepreneur, author, and professional speaker. He firmly believes that everyone has the potential to be creative and achieve personal goals by developing solid habits and following learnable methods. He has taught these methods at conventions, in classrooms, and to companies. He has trained multiple successful designers within his own companies, many of whom have gone on to have hugely successful careers in the game industry.

Justin started his career in gaming at the age of seventeen when he won the *Magic: The Gathering* US National Championships. He went on to play *Magic* professionally for several years, winning a Grand Prix, Pro Tour, and World Championship along the way. Justin started designing games working on the *Vs. System* trading card game and went on to lead-design the *DC Comics: Infinite Crisis* set. Afterwards, he created the *World of Warcraft Miniatures* game before starting his own company, Gary Games, in 2010, which released the hit deck-building game *Ascension* that year.

Justin and his games have been featured in news outlets across the globe, including *The New York Times, Fortune Magazine,*

Forbes, Inc., Wired, The Seattle Met, The Miami Herald, The San Francisco Chronicle, and even *Playboy TV!* During his twenty years in the gaming industry, Justin has been invited to speak at numerous conventions and industry events, including Gen Con, SXSW, Origins, and the Penny Arcade Expo.

Justin's passion for speaking began at an early age when he joined (and eventually captained) his high school and college debate teams. His love for teaching also began there, and it continued with his teaching of the Kaplan LSAT course and several guest lectures at universities and schools to teach the art of game design.

Originally from Miami, Florida, Justin graduated with honors from Dartmouth College with a BA in Philosophy in 2002. He now designs games, consults, and runs multiple successful companies from his home in San Diego, California.

GAMES DESIGNED BY THE AUTHOR

Ascension Deckbuilding Game—Stone Blade Entertainment
Bad Beets—Stone Blade Entertainment
Dungeon Draft—Upper Deck Entertainment
Hero 108: Kingdom Crashers—Playmates
Redakai Trading Card Game—Spin Master
Shards of Infinity—Stone Blade Entertainment
SolForge Digital Collectible Card Game—Stone Blade Entertainment
The Breakthrough Game—Wharton School of Business
The Startup Game—Wharton School of Business
Vs. System DC Trading Card Game—Upper Deck Entertainment
Vs. System Marvel Trading Card Game—Upper Deck Entertainment
World of Warcraft Miniatures Game—Upper Deck Entertainment
You Gotta Be Kitten Me—Stone Blade Entertainment

STONE BLADE ENTERTAINMENT

Founded by Justin Gary in 2010 as Gary Games, Stone Blade Entertainment publishes tabletop and digital games for passionate gamers and their friends and family. These are the games we want to play and love to share with the world.

Beginning with the hugely successful *Ascension* deck-building game, Stone Blade Entertainment has since published over a dozen *Ascension* expansions, as well as launching many other games for both digital and tabletop form. These games include *SolForge Digital Collectible Card Game*, *Shards of Infinity* deckbuilding game, *Bad Beets* bluffing card game, and *You Gotta Be Kitten Me* party card game.

You can check out more games from Stone Blade Entertainment at its website www.stoneblade.com and stay up to date by following its Facebook page https://www.Facebook.com/StoneBladeEnt/.

ABOUT GAMER ENTERTAINMENT

Gamer Entertainment has been providing design consulting services for over a decade. Founded by Justin Gary in 2008, Gamer Entertainment has provided support for countless projects of all sizes around the world. Previous clients include the Wharton School of Business, Playmates, Hasbro, MySpace, and Spin Master. Gamer Entertainment offers everything from gamification consulting and design evaluations to full-scale implementations of designs in the tabletop, digital, and educational spaces.

Gamer Entertainment's mission is to provide world-class design services to make the world more inspiring and entertaining. Justin has assembled a team of dozens of incredible designers trained in the principles outlined in this book. If you are interested in consulting services for your game or business project, sign up for a complimentary thirty-minute consultation at:

www.GamerEntertainment.com

MORE LESSONS

For those of you hungry for more lessons from some of the brightest minds in game design, I've got you covered. After publishing this book, I began working on a series of projects to support our growing community of game designers.

You can find all the resources and more at justingary.com

ACKNOWLEDGMENTS

There are so many people I owe thanks to it will be impossible to list them all here. I have been blessed my entire life with incredible friends, family, and coworkers who have taught me so much and made me into who I am today.

To my beautiful, kind, loving, and wonderful girlfriend Cece: You have been a safe harbor for me from which I can venture out into uncharted waters. Your support has meant the world to me, and your belief in my ability and your willingness to listen to my half-baked ideas has inspired me to ever more incredible achievements. But the greatest achievement of all has been the happiness we've found in our life together.

To my family: We are an eclectic bunch and I love you all. My siblings Jon, George, Brooke, Zach, and Abbey all challenged me in our friendly (and sometimes not-so-friendly) games and harnessed my competitive edge. I am grateful to my stepfather Michael Snyder for making my mom so happy, and for uniting our two families into a unified whole. Your advice and counsel over the years have helped me immensely.

To Gary Arant: When I hired you, I only knew you as a clever kid from the local card shop. Since then, I have watched you grow into an incredible designer, leader, and father. Your talent, commitment, and brilliance have been responsible for so much of our success, and I am forever grateful. Seeing your growth, humility, and commitment to excellence continues to inspire me. I am proud to have played a small role in helping you along your path.

To the rest of Stone Blade Entertainment's team, investors, and partners: Everything I've built has been on the foundation of your hard work, brilliance, resourcefulness, and ingenuity. I'm proud to lead such an incredible group and proud of the independent accomplishments of everyone who has gone on to bigger and better things. So many people are required to build the kinds of things we build, and my greatest skill has been to surround myself with incredible people who inspire me to be better. There are far too many of you to name here, but please know that I am thankful for each and every one of you, regardless of where you are today.

To my friends, society brothers, and rave family: I finally wrote that book I've been talking about for so long, and I owe much of it to all of you. Thanks for holding me accountable and inspiring me with your own accomplishments. Thank you for showing me my blind spots, helping me get over my failures, and celebrating my successes. You all continue to remind me what is important in life, and I couldn't be happier to be on this journey together.